Dedications

To my wife, **Hamsa Ramaswamy**, whose love, support, and sacrifices have made my dreams a reality. To my critics and 2 outstanding storytellers, **Vidhubala Vasudevan** and **Meena Vasudevan**, who also happen to be my daughters. I love you girls to the moon and back.

Contents

Preface

Actress Savithri died in 1981. I was 3 years old then. She was my mother's favorite actress, and upon hearing the news of her demise, my mother walked for over a kilometer from home with me in her arms to buy the evening newspaper and learn more about what happened to Savithri. My father, who returned from the office then, was surprised to see the house locked. Thinking my mother should have gone out on some urgency, he waited outside the door for 30 minutes with no clue of my mother's whereabouts.

My father was surprised and angry 😊 when my mother came home weeping with a newspaper in hand and started sharing details of the actress' death, utterly oblivious to my father's state of mind 😊. I think my love for movies is something I genetically inherited from my mother.

I was fascinated by actors, directors, editors, writers, and everybody associated with the industry. I read so much about what happened on and off the screen when a movie was made by reading magazines as a kid. As I grew up, I watched many movies and learned from them. More than movies, movie making got my attention. The effort that went into making a movie inspired me. I learned so much about project management from movie making in areas like Project Planning, Scope Management,

Schedule Management, Time Management, Cost Management, Quality Management, Risk, and Communication Management.

So, I started 'Movie Monday' with the goal of inspiring fellow Zucians and helping them find their true potential by sharing stories from the world of cinema. Today, 'Movie Monday' has grown into an inspirational weekly email that reaches 500+ Zucians who are passionate about leadership, self-improvement, and everyday betterment.

I am very thankful to our Head of Corporate Communications, **Satish Chathanath**, for coming up with the idea to convert the weekly 'Movie Monday' emails into a book and for bringing the concept to fruition. I thank my co-founders, **Anil Kumar Sannareddy** and **Venkatesh Veerachamy,** for their constant support and motivation. My thanks to all Zucians for their responses, encouragement, and support.

I hope you enjoy reading this.

About the Author

Vasudevan Swaminathan, the Founder and CEO of Zuci Systems, is a seasoned storyteller who seamlessly combines his passion for cinema with his expertise in corporate strategy. Vasudevan's background in business management and his appreciation for the silver screen have enabled him to explore the intersection of storytelling, leadership, and innovation. His extensive immersion in both corporate dynamics and the entertainment industry has enriched his writing with a distinct and insightful perspective.

As the author of *Random Takes*, Vasudevan vividly illustrates the transformative potential of storytelling within the business realm. Through his compelling examination of iconic films and their intricate behind-the-scenes processes, he unveils actionable insights and pioneering strategies for leaders and teams to leverage the emotional resonance of storytelling effectively. Vasudevan's discerning eye for detail and his fervent commitment to uncovering untapped opportunities infuse his work with a fresh outlook on leadership and business strategy.

In addition to his literary pursuits, Vasudevan is a highly sought-after speaker and accomplished corporate executive renowned for his dynamic presentations and strategic prowess. Whether captivating audiences from the podium or through his

LinkedIn articles, Vasudevan inspires individuals to reimagine their approach to leadership and business, harnessing the enduring wisdom of cinema to instigate meaningful change and foster profound connections in the corporate landscape.

Enable. Empower. Exemplify.

The **American Film Institute (AFI)** honors film industry veterans yearly, and I love the speeches and tributes showered by other artists who shared screen space with the awardee. One such speech I always like and revisit is what actress Jodie Foster did for Robert De Niro. For me, this is a classic example of a leadership trait that Ms. Foster talks about. ***Why is it a key leadership trait?*** Good leaders play 2 critical roles. In the task-oriented role, *the leader ensures that members have the knowledge, training, skills, and discipline to execute their tasks well and that they get done.* In mentoring, *the leader chooses the best people, blends their talent and expertise, and helps them manage their interpersonal relationships. Robert De Niro knows that.*

Clive Lloyd captained the West Indies team during the 1970s. He was not an exceptional batsman or bowler and could never be one, *for greats like Vivian Richards and Gordon Greenidge surrounded him.* But Clive Lloyd was the greatest leadership material that could have happened to the Windies. Some call him the most excellent captain ever. **Why**? There are many reasons, but mainly: ***Clive Lloyd brought together a diverse collection of talented individuals from different Caribbean islands who lacked direction, focus, discipline, mental toughness, and common purpose and transformed them into a highly professional, disciplined, and all-conquering unit that***

dominated the world cricket for more than 15 years. Clive had a clear and powerful vision of what he wanted his team to achieve and become. *He imprinted that vision into his players' minds and showed them how they would benefit from achieving the team's goals.*

Some other names that come to my mind immediately on the same lines as Clive Lloyd are **Sourav Ganguly**, **Steve Waugh**, **Mahendra Singh Dhoni,** and **Arjuna Ranatunga**. They were not superstars like Don Bradman, Sachin Tendulkar, or Brian Lara, but they had great leadership traits, mainly when it came to identifying and nurturing talent. And that's precisely what Robert De Niro had. Jodie Foster says, *"Robert De Niro took it upon himself to introduce her to the craft of acting."* To quote her verbatim, *"I had spent 9 years in the industry, but no one bothered to teach me what acting was, but Bob did."* **Good leaders play the role of mentors.** They are coaches. They see potential and talent and bring them to the front. All the names I mentioned above in the world of cricket did that. Clive Lloyd never took credit for what he did to the West Indies team but was just **'enabling'** and **'empowering'** every team player by being the team's crux and bringing them all together. In the process, he **'exemplified'** leadership.

What Matters More: Chalk or a Clean Slate?

When we decided to bootstrap Zuci in 2016, I contacted a highly qualified academician friend in the US. I requested that he put me in touch with his friend, an entrepreneur who had founded a successful business. My friend made the introductions, and I was ready to meet this gentleman at a Starbucks. I had no business or entrepreneurship knowledge, but I only had 17 years of software industry experience working in different capacities. Basically, I was a "clean slate" when it came to running a business.

As the talk continued, I recognized that he was highlighting some of my vulnerabilities, like my lack of preparedness regarding my limited business management skills, lack of a comprehensive financial strategy, lack of backup plans in case the firm failed, etc. In essence, he was saying, "You don't seem to be prepared suitably, and entrepreneurship has a definite road to be followed to meet with success."

As I left the meeting, thanking him for his time and input, I saw a big smile all over his face, the one that said, "I saved the business world from another excited but unprepared entrepreneur who for sure would have embarrassed the successful ones." ☺

I am glad that I did not take his input, or else I would have ended up trying to build a plan, a business plan canvas, and other strategic items and doubting my abilities.

The 'Conventional Wisdom' (a widely held notion or belief) advises that you take the route that has been successful for others. From sales, marketing, technology, HR, and everything else, people want to follow well-established practices and processes so they don't fail. No one wants to 'defy conventional wisdom' because it is risky, there is no guarantee for success, and when you fail, you are at the crux of all the blame because you decided to take the road less traveled. No one is exempt from this, not even the film industry. People want everyone to follow the same path others have taken because it has led to success for others. For example, heroes avoid trying different roles because they don't want to risk their image. Directors tend to write scripts that guarantee "minimum income" from the trade. Producers want directors to follow the same approach that worked for a recent film, which turned out to be a blockbuster hit.

Is it wrong to believe what is widely believed? Why ignore it? Perhaps 'Dev D,' 'Gangs of Wasseypur,' 'Raman Raghav 2.0', and 'Manmarziyaan' filmmaker Anurag Kashyap can provide an answer. Young Anurag Kashyap had to pick between 'conventional wisdom knowledge' and 'challenging it' in 1995, and he decided to do the latter. Why? Let's hear it from him directly:

"I was 22 years old, and, I signed a contract with Mahesh Bhatt. The great Bhatt Saab whose contract for writing a daily soap, which was called 'Kabhi Kabhi' would give me 2.5 lacs a month. This was, back in 1995. I was 22 then. And, at the same

time, I was approached for the film "Satya," where the deal was "we cannot pay you more than Rs.10,000 a month, and, not more than 10 months." And, that was the hard choice. That was the choice, and Mahesh Bhatt's contract was one month old. I had just started to make money and started getting credit and I got a film which had no certainty, which would not pay me more than Rs.10,000 a month, not for more than 10 months and that film took 3 years of my life.

So, those are the choices that somehow, in life take you along. And for those 3 years, every time I met someone including my own family would say, "what's wrong with you?" "Finally, you wanted to do something, and you are making money" But, sometimes you feel like 'this is not' what you want in life. I don't want to be one of those coxes in a wheel that moves as things move. You want to do something. I had a certain Idea that the cinema that inspired me, that I saw in 1993 is the kind of cinema I wanted to create. And that cinema was not being made.

If I would have stuck to making money writing for soaps and all that, I would never do that. I would be a part of the same system. And, I wanted to go out and change things and, we wanted to disrupt systems. And I found a Ram Gopal Verma, who was disrupting the system. He was an outsider who came in, who did not care, whose whole life was about movies. And, while working with him for 3 years, I learned how he made films, how he made a movie like Satya. Nobody wanted to make Satya."

Defying conventional wisdom for the sake of it is not needed, but to help break stereotypes and innovate, it is required. Whether we code, sell, position the brand, or hire, we talk about 'thinking out of the box' and thinking out of the box is nothing but defying conventional wisdom.

I believe our future is always a blank slate. Not just every quarter of the year but every day of every quarter.

Stay in Character and Get Remarkable Outcomes

A testing business from Israel contacted me to write blog posts for a project they are developing for the tester community around 2021. They seem to have read my blogs from Sticky Minds and other forums and thought my contribution could be of use to their readers. I was offered $60 for every blog article that I submitted. I was thrilled, not for the money but for the fact that someone was willing to pay me for what I liked doing. They considered my writing skills 'attractive'. Your skill is your competitive advantage, isn't it? Looking back, I started writing in 2005, but for the most part, I borrowed content from multiple sources and used it since I was struggling to put my thoughts on paper. Between 2005 and 2017, I produced 1-2 articles per year, but I was not very good at it. During the next 2 years, I increased my writing. I can say that I have written roughly about 100-150 articles across topics between 2019 and 2020. My point is that my writing skills have improved only during the past 3-4 years after I started writing more. I could have spent more time honing my writing skills, but I didn't. I was lazy, and I continue to be. ☺

'Honing your craft' is extremely important, but many of us have no idea how to do it. How can you improve your programming skills? How can you improve your sales or marketing skills? How can you develop your HR expertise?

———••———

Of course, the simple answer to these questions is 'practice,' but how can we practice to become better programmers and sales/marketing/HR professionals? The truth is, we don't get to solve complex problems every day as a programmer or put our sales skills to use to win a deal where 4 competitors are vying for the same thing. We can probably get some cues on this topic from the movie industry, particularly from method actors. Now, try applying the same question to actors. How can you practice to become a better actor? They are no different from a sales/marketing/HR professional. You can get trained in some general skills such as horse riding, stunts, etc, but you don't get trained to play the saxophone unless there is a role that comes to you where you need to play the instrument.

Method actors like Marlon Brando, Daniel Day-Lewis, Robert De Niro, Jack Nicholson, Christian Bale, and many others surprise us with their acting skills because we don't see them in the characters they play. For instance, consider Christian Bale. Watch *American Psycho,* and he scares us. He shed 63 lbs for *The Machinist* in 2004, gained 100 lbs, and bulked up for *Batman Begins* 6 months later. And he goes to play a totally different character in *The Big Short*, and then he transforms himself to play Dick Cheney in *Vice*, for which he gained 40lbs and wore prosthetics. How does Christian Bale train for these kinds of roles? How does he hone his acting skills? Most actors say, "They start preparing for the character from the time they hear the script and stay in the character until the shoot gets over, even if that takes 2 years.

"Staying in character" means "continuous preparation" or "honing their craft" to play the character. They walk, talk, and behave as the characters inside and outside the sets. They deeply immerse themselves in the role, trying to understand the various dimensions of the character and how the character would behave or react in a particular situation. Now, that kind of deep dive and preparation may not be possible for all of us, but we can "stay in character," too. All it means to us is "looking at the details more carefully instead of being superficially engaged."

Going the extra mile and writing some more unit testing code is the programmer's approach to "staying in character." 😊 An intense research about a prospect for 60 minutes and preparing to surprise them with their business challenges and the way to solve them is the salesperson's way of "staying in character." 😊 If we are looking for examples, look at Elon Musk. Elon Musk had no prior knowledge of rockets or space travel, but over time, he gradually gained all of it.

Space experts claim that he learned all of them by reading books and that he is now qualified to consult with specialists on every part of the rocket. Elon Musk has been "staying in character" every day for the past 18+ years as far as "SpaceX" goes. 😊

Continuous preparation is like having a continuous supply of oxygen when you are climbing a professional mountain.

Hope is a Good Thing, and No Good Thing Ever Dies

There is an old Zen tale about a monarch whose subjects had become petty and entitled. Dissatisfied with this situation, the king hoped to teach them a lesson. His plan was simple: he placed a large boulder in the middle of the main road, blocking entry into the city. He chose to hide nearby and observe their reactions. How would they respond? Would they cooperate to take it out? Or would they give up, become dejected, and go back home? The king observed with increasing despair as subject after subject approached this obstruction and walked away. Or, at best, tried half-heartedly before giving up. After several days, a lone peasant came along on his way into town. He didn't veer off. In fact, he exerted some effort to get it out of the way. Then, a thought struck him. He scrambled into the nearby woods to find something he could use for leverage. Finally, he returned with a large branch he had made into a lever and used it to dislodge the massive rock out of the way. Beneath the rock was a purse of gold coins and a note from the king, which said: **"The obstacle in the path becomes the path. Never forget, within every obstacle is an opportunity to improve our condition."**

The great men and women of this world didn't have exceptional luck, talent, or experience. **They only followed one rule of life: "What stands in the way becomes the way."** You can apply this to Gandhi, Nelson Mandela, Steve Jobs, and many others. This idea derives from "Stoicism," a Greek philosophy of life that maximizes positive emotions, reduces negative emotions, and helps individuals hone their virtues of character. The book *The Obstacle Is The Way: The Ancient Art of Turning Adversity to Benefit* by Ryan Holiday was my introduction to Stoicism.

Stoicism asks us to focus on the moment and not the monsters that may or may not be up ahead. In one of the chapters, Ryan Holiday discusses this by using instances of businesses that were founded during an economic downturn. He asserts that a bear market or recession is when half of the Fortune 500 businesses are founded. Literally, half. This is the list:

Proctor & Gamble (Panic of 1837)

General Motors (Panic of 1907)

UPS (Panic of 1907)

Walt Disney Company (After 11 months of smooth operation, the 12th was the market crash of 1929)

Fortune Magazine (90 days after the market crash of 1929)

Revlon (Great Depression, 1932)

HP (Great Depression, 1935)

Costco (recession in the late 1970's)

FedEx (oil crisis of 1973)

Microsoft (recession in 1973-75)

LinkedIn (2002, post-dot-com bubble)

The point is that most people start from a disadvantage (often with no idea they are doing so) and do just fine. It's not unfair; it's universal. **Those who survive it survive because they take things day by day – that's the real secret.**

The Stoic philosophy is all around us and in the movies we watch. *Gladiator, The Godfather, Cinderella Man, Rocky, Dunkirk, Spartacus,* and *Ben-Hur* are some of the movies with Stoic elements. One of my favorite movies, *The Shawshank Redemption*, has a lot of Stoicism to offer. The lead character of the movie, Andy Dufresne, carries a lot of Stoic qualities. We need to understand the plot of the movie in order to comprehend Andy and his stoic demeanor.

Smart banker Andy Dufresne is falsely charged with killing his wife and her lover. He is given a life sentence in the severely fortified prison of Shawshank. Andy befriends Ellis Boyd Redding (Red), who remains his ally throughout the story. Andy's intentions and his mental posture remain unclear at first. Like others, he grapples with the daily hardships of prison life. But what makes him stand apart from the rest is his attitude toward those hardships and how he endures them with a smile on his face. Andy faces numerous challenges put forth by the negative characters in the movie. However, he manages to maintain a calm demeanor while pacing slowly (and steadily) toward his goal of escaping prison. It takes Andy years in his cell to discreetly dig the hole to freedom. And the D-day finally arrives. With sheer hard work and luck on his side, Andy executes his plan. He escapes from Shawshank after 19 years of jail time — defeating all his enemies once and for all. The story ends with Red being set free and meeting Andy in a far-off destination, where they live together thereafter.

Andy Dufresne finds meaning through suffering. **Isn't that what a lot of people in the world have found during COVID-19 times?** The movie says, "Keep a laser focus on your target and achieve it no matter what circumstances you are in." Even your freedom can be taken away, but, in Andy's words, **"There is something inside you that can't be taken away."**

Do Emotions Oppose Rational Thought?

I recently had the opportunity to meet one of our clients. We had lunch together, and some of the life lessons he imparted were both interesting and inspiring. He underwent a kidney transplant when he was 43 years old (I estimate that he is now between 55 and 60 years old), and despite being informed that running would be bad for his health, he has been competing in marathons for many years. If I remember correctly, his brother used to run backwards, and he currently holds the third spot or mentions in the Guinness Book of Records for the longest marathon runner backward. Participation in marathon athletic events runs in the family, and he has done one with his son recently. Mostly, he participates in marathons that are for social causes. He is a good man and spoke about many other things, including his personal life. From the different incidents he shared from his life, what struck me the most was when he said he has stopped judging people and wants to live a life that is of help to others.

I kept thinking about it. Stephen Covey's book *The 7 Habits of Highly Effective People* and the Disney movie *Inside Out* came to mind. In his book, Stephen Covey asks readers to look at the image below and say whether they see a "young lady" or an "old woman" in the picture.

This exercise is to demonstrate clearly that 2 people can see the same thing, disagree, and yet both be right. It's not logical, it's psychological. Stephen Covey says we are conditioned to see things in our own way and how powerfully conditioning affects our perceptions. He uses the "perception demonstration" image below because it yields so many insights into both personal and interpersonal effectiveness. How many of you can see the young woman, how many can see the elderly woman, and how many can see both of them? 😊

Some famous movies about the "nature of human perception" are *Rashomon* (the famous "Rashomon Effect" comes from this), *A History of Violence*, *Memento*, *Mulholland Drive*, *The Usual Suspects*, *Virumandi* (Tamil Movie), and many others.

On the other hand, Disney's *Inside Out*, which came out in 2015, is about how 5 emotions — personified as the characters Anger, Disgust, Fear, Sadness, and Joy — grapple for control of the mind of an 11-year-old girl named Riley during the tumult of a move from Minnesota to San Francisco. **Traditionally, in**

the history of Western thought, the prevailing view has been that emotions are enemies of rationality and disruptive of cooperative social relations. But the truth is that emotions guide our perceptions of the world, our memories of the past, and even our moral judgments of right and wrong, most typically in ways that enable effective responses to the current situation. Studies have shown, for example, that when we are angry, we are too focused on the unfairness part. This can make us want to do awful things to make things right.

In conclusion, many confrontations could be resolved much more amicably if we could see things from the perspective of the other party, but regrettably, our "conditioning" doesn't allow us to do that. ☺

Happy Endings

I had a memorable discussion with Sridhar Vembu of Zoho Corp as part of our "Soorarai Potru" intiative (which is renamed as THE Z TALK) at Zuci Systems. Sridhar's company had 150 clients, and the dot-com bubble reduced it to just 3. A lot of people left the company, and amidst the harrowing times, Sridhar told me that he used to come to the office every day, which to him resembled a "funeral house." Sridhar did not lose faith but was also not oblivious to the current reality. He started building "Advent Net" from there before it became what is called "ZOHO" today.

One of the best illustrations of the "Stockdale Paradox" is shown above.

In the best-selling book by Jim Collins, *Good to Great*, one of the 6 ingredients that "good" companies used to become "great" was to **confront the brutal facts (yet never lose faith)—also known as the Stockdale Paradox.**

In the corporate world, the Stockdale Paradox is a strategy to get through difficult and ambiguous times by combining the capacity to face the harsh realities of your present situation while maintaining unflinching trust that you will succeed in the end, no matter how distant that is.

Jim Collins came up with this concept, "Stockdale Paradox," named after Admiral James Stockdale, one of the most decorated United States Navy officers, who was also awarded the Medal of Honor in the Vietnam War.

Stockdale's story is extreme. He was leading a mission in North Vietnam when his plane was shot down, and he ejected and parachuted into enemy territory. As a prisoner of war from 1965 to 1973, Stockdale was tortured over 20 times, had no prisoner's rights, no release date, and no idea whether he would survive to see his family again. Yet, he survived when many of his co-prisoners didn't. **What was his secret?**

First, Stockdale had absolute faith and belief that he would get out. However, Stockdale didn't depend on naive optimism alone. **Ironically, none of his fellow inmates survived, even the one who was the most optimistic.** Precisely because they were so hopeful that their ordeal would be over soon, they were disappointed to find themselves still in captivity when Christmas came, then Easter, then Thanksgiving, then the next Christmas, and at the end, they lost all hope and eventually "died of a broken heart." Stockdale, on the other hand, was fully aware of his dire circumstances and made every effort to increase his chances of survival.

Stockdale described his approach. Here is the important lesson in his own words: "You must never confuse faith that you will prevail in the end—which you can never afford to lose—with the discipline to confront the most brutal facts of your current reality, whatever they might be." - Admiral James Stockdale.

The only way to become great is to persevere despite suffering and uncertainty.

Do you recall Om Kapoor's acclaimed speech from *Om Shanti Om*? "Just like in films, in life too, we all need "happy endings," and if it's not a "happy ending', the film has not yet ended." He adds, "To me, that **"Picture abhi baaki hai mere dost."** is our take on the "reality of the moment" while we wait for "happy endings." 😊

Coma to a Masterclass

In 1993, an elderly man named Eugene Pauly was rushed to an emergency room near San Diego, suffering from stomach cramps, vomiting, and a high 105-degree temperature. It turned out that Eugene was suffering from encephalitis, which affects the brain. He slipped into a coma for 10 days, and when he woke up, his wife Beverly was forced to face the fact that Eugene was no longer the same. Although he could still speak, he could no longer remember the day of the week, had trouble recalling conversations, and frequently prepared his own breakfast without really eating it before falling asleep and repeating the process later.

Coming to terms with reality, Eugene and Beverly moved to a new area to be close to their daughter, and one of the important parts of his daily routine was a walk around the block. The doctors told Beverly that she had to monitor her husband constantly - if he ever got lost, he would never be able to find his way back home. After all, he was unable to tell you which door in his living room led to the kitchen. One morning, Beverley got dressed before their morning walk as usual. She then went to find Eugene and couldn't find him. He had disappeared. Terrified, Beverly ran around the neighborhood, screaming his name, but couldn't find him. **Distraught and not knowing what else to do, she went home to find her husband watching the**

history channel. On the table lay a pile of pinecones that he had collected on his walk.

How did he do it? Repetition. When a task is repeated enough times, a process known as "chunking" occurs in which the brain turns a series of deliberate acts into a pattern that runs automatically.

"If you repeat an action often enough, it will become automatic and therefore effortless." - The Pauly Principle.

The brain loves shortcuts. We can only remember 7 pieces of information with our conscious minds, so once we learn any skill, that knowledge gets stored in the subconscious, where we can recall it automatically. The ability to read the very words in this email is a skill you learned consciously and with effort at school, but that is now completely effortless. The reason the brain loves shortcuts is that it knows they are good for survival. Whatever you keep repeating, the brain will make it automatic. It even worked for a man with extensively damaged brain functioning. Eugene Pauly became the subject of intense study by neuroscientists because he overshot the potential they expected to see in anyone who had suffered this level of brain damage. He is a masterclass in how habits really become effortless and automatic.

I came to know of Eugene Pauly and **"The Pauly Principle" from Charles Duhigg's book *The Power of Habit*.** There is a TEDx talk from Charles Duhigg on the "Power of Habit."

Reading about "The Pauly Principle" reminded me of *Forrest Gump*, which is one of the best movies of all time. The 1994 film starring Tom Hanks tells the story of a kind-hearted man from Alabama who, despite having a low IQ, manages to accomplish great things while also positively influencing the lives of those around him. **In *The Power of Habit*, Charles Duhigg explains that success often requires performing quiet, boring, and repetitive tasks.** By performing such tasks, you gain mastery. That is what Forrest Gump did.

What Can Brick Walls Teach Us?

Randy Pausch was an American educator and a professor of computer science, human-computer interaction, and design at Carnegie Mellon University (CMU) in Pittsburgh, Pennsylvania. Pausch learned he had pancreatic cancer in September 2006. In August 2007, he was given a terminal diagnosis: **"3 to 6 months of good health left"** (read: time left to live).

On September 18, 2007, at Carnegie Mellon, Randy Pausch presented a motivational speech titled **"The Last Lecture: Truly Achieving Your Childhood Dreams"** that went viral on YouTube and led to other media appearances. On July 25, 2008, Pausch, then 47, passed away because of pancreatic cancer complications.

Though I enjoyed Randy's entire presentation, there is one section in particular that I always listen to when "my chips are down," and that is about how to overcome brick walls. What is a "brick wall"? A brick wall is variously used as a metaphor for a challenging obstacle or obstruction. And what is Randy's take on brick walls? He says, "Brick walls are there for a reason. The brick walls are not there to keep us out. The brick walls are there to show how badly we want something. Because the brick walls are there to stop the people who do not want something badly enough, they are there to keep out the other people."

Nearly every time Randy faces a challenge, he calls it a "brick wall." However, rather than letting these brick walls keep him from what he wants, Randy uses the walls as opportunities to show how badly he wants whatever it is that they are blocking. **Brick walls try to stop Randy from getting accepted to Brown University, floating in NASA's zero gravity machine, becoming a Disney Imagineer, and wooing Jai, his future wife.** Each time, Randy faces a challenge that prevents him from achieving his goals, but he is unfazed by them. In fact, as he looks back on his life, he realizes that each of these hurdles was put in place for a reason because they "give us a chance to show how much we want something."

The section of Randy's talk titled "Brick Wall" wonderfully explains the true meaning of failure and struggle. At times, we all struggle with life and fail. We all do, sometimes major and other times modest. It is so easy to give up during those times or to make justifications for why we aren't smart, capable, or deserving enough. **The alternative is to understand that failing does not make you a failure and that how you respond to failure depends entirely on your way of thinking.**

The 2011 feature film *Soul Surfer* captures the story of Bethany Hamilton and how she overcame the brick walls in her life. Bethany Hamilton is an American professional surfer who hit a "brick wall" in 2003 when her left arm was bitten off by a shark during surfing. Despite the trauma of the incident, Hamilton was determined to return to surfing. One month after the attack, she returned to her board, and she ultimately returned to professional surfing.

What are the brick walls at which you are currently staring? What stops you from breaking them, scaling them, or weakening them? Just take action.

When We Change Our Attitude, Sparks Fly in the Universe.

In the film *The Theory of Everything*, which chronicles the life of theoretical physicist Stephen Hawking, this is one of my favorite quotes:

"There should be no boundaries to human endeavor. We are all different. However bad life may seem, there is always something you can do and succeed at. While there is life, there is hope." - Stephen Hawking.

Hawking was diagnosed shortly after his 21st birthday as suffering from an unspecified incurable disease, which was then identified as the fatal degenerative motor neuron disease amyotrophic lateral sclerosis, or ALS. Rather than succumbing to depression, as most people might have done, Hawking began to set sights on some of the most fundamental questions concerning the physical nature of the universe. In due course, he achieved extraordinary success against the severest physical disabilities. **Defying all medical opinions, including being given "2 weeks to live" when he was first diagnosed with ALS, he managed to live another 55 years.**

The Diving Bell and the Butterfly is another true story-based film that demonstrates how your attitude can help you achieve everything you set your mind to.

On December 8, 1995, while taking his kid to the theater, a 43-year-old journalist and editor of the French fashion magazine *Elle*, Jean-Dominique Bauby, experienced a cerebrovascular seizure. **When he woke up in the hospital 20 days later, he could only blink his left eyelid.** He was suffering from locked-in syndrome, in which the mental faculties remain intact, but most of the body is paralyzed.

Before his seizure, Bauby had signed a contract to write a book. His speech therapist, Sandrine Fichou, arranged a 26-letter alphabet according to frequency of use so that Bauby could dictate. Claude Mendibil, a ghostwriter and freelance book editor, was sent by his publisher, Robert Laffont, to take the dictation using a system called partner-assisted scanning. She recited the alphabet until Bauby blinked at the correct letter and recorded the 130-page manuscript, letter by letter, over the course of 2 months, working 3 hours a day, 7 days a week. The resulting book, The Diving Bell and the Butterfly was published in 1997.

This is not just about Stephen Hawking and Jean-Dominique Bauby, whom the world came to know. There are several other people who live in such conditions, like Nick Chisolm, whose happy face while living with locked-in syndrome is something I often visit to tell myself, "Don't complain; you are not living the life of Nick Chisolm." The author Jeff Keller writes in his book *Attitude is Everything*: "You see, when you change your attitude, sparks fly in the universe. **You are energized. You begin to see new possibilities. You move into action. You achieve**

extraordinary results. That is why I say when you change your attitude, you change your life!"

Stephen Hawking, Jean-Dominique Bauby, and Nick Chisolm are all examples of Jeff Keller's words above.

In the business world, what is more powerful than a power suit? – Your positive attitude! When you wear it, you see sparks fly in the universe.

Strength is More Mental Than Physical

Sachin Tendulkar's 241-run knock at the SCG is arguably the most disciplined innings ever in the history of Test cricket! What makes it so special? Sachin got out twice during that 1999 tour of Australia playing cover drives, and before the next test match, he said he was not going to play any cover drives. **He scored a massive 241 runs in the next test match with "zero" cover drives.**

Sportspersons often have muscle memory, especially someone like Sachin, who has been playing for years. When the ball is bowled outside off, going for a cover drive is automatic and instinctual. To not give into that instinct for 431 balls takes some seriously amazing mental strength and discipline.

When we talk of mental toughness, *127 Hours* springs to mind.

Danny Boyle's *127 Hours* is about the story of mechanical engineer Aron Ralston, who worked for Intel. On April 26, 2003, Aron Ralston was canyoneering in Utah. While he was descending the lower stretches of the canyon, a suspended boulder dislodged while he was climbing down from it. The boulder first smashed his left hand and then crushed his right hand against the canyon wall. After being trapped for 6 days and trying all sorts of ways to free himself and drinking his own urine in order to survive without food and water, he finally decided to break his bone and amputate his arm with the help of a small pocket knife and managed to free himself from the narrow place where he had been stuck for days.

One of the most extraordinary survival stories ever told—Aron Ralston's account of 6 days trapped in one of the most remote spots in America and how one inspired act of bravery brought him home—was turned into a book titled *Between a Rock and a Hard Place*, which Danny Boyle made into a movie. Aron Ralston's story has 2 key lessons for us:

- Strength is more mental than physical. **We can come out of the most terrible situations if we have resilience in us.** Difficult times are part of life and sometimes unavoidable. We can either see it as a problem or as an opportunity to discover our hidden strengths; the choice is always ours.

- You have to help yourself. **Not in every situation will you find others to help you. Don't quit even if there's no one around, and eventually, you will find the right people.**

Who You Surround Yourself With Matters

President Abraham Lincoln decided to fill his cabinet with political adversaries, namely the men who ran against him in the contentious 1860 election. Lincoln's explanation for this decision was that the country needed the strongest, most capable men to lead it; collectively, these men could offer that. From Lincoln's perspective, just because they had been bitter rivals during the election didn't justify depriving the country of their talents and leadership.

If you are building a team anywhere in your life or business, ask yourself, **"Am I looking to surround myself with the 'most capable' people, or am I looking for individuals who would say 'Yes' to everything I do?"** Ray Dalio, legendary investor, founder of Bridgewater Associates, and author of one of the most invaluable leadership books, Principles, writes about the importance of building a team that is comfortable with conflict and challenging each other. He also addresses the danger of confirmation bias, born from surrounding ourselves with people who tell us what we want to hear. Dalio believes that "The greatest tragedy of mankind comes from the inability of people to have thoughtful disagreement to find out what's true."

Surrounding themselves with people who are capable but challenging to work with is very common in the film industry. Marlon Brando (*The Godfather*, *On the Waterfront*) is considered a very difficult actor to work with, as he would often improvise scenes without any prior notice and make the other actors in the scene uncomfortable. Daniel Day-Lewis (*Lincoln*, *There Will Be Blood*, *Gangs of New York*) stays in character throughout the duration of the movie and expects others to treat him as the character and not as Daniel Day-Lewis, causing annoyance to the film cast and crew. Edward Norton (*The Incredible Hulk*, *Birdman*, *Fight Club*) constantly shares thoughts with directors on how they can craft a scene better, leading to tiffs and quarrels on the sets. But these actors deliver terrific performances that get etched into the walls of film history.

Like Lincoln, **the best leaders triangulate their views with believable people who are willing to disagree and challenge their closely held assumptions and beliefs.** They do this because they want to significantly raise the probability of the best outcome or decision.

Intuition or Logic?

On a cold day in January 2009, US Airways flight 1549 took off from New York's La Guardia airport toward Charlotte with 155 people on board. Captain Chesley Sullenberger (a.k.a. Sully) was in command. It was yet another day for Sully at work. As a former fighter pilot, he had an impeccable record of flying. However, this flight proved to be the ultimate test of his flying career.

Soon after takeoff, a flock of birds hit the aircraft, damaging both engines. The Air Traffic Controller at La Guardia directed the captain to return to base. The aircraft was steadily losing altitude, and Sully knew instantly that he wouldn't make it back to the airport. ***He had less than 3 minutes to "make some kind of decision" before the plane went down.*** Setting aside his panic, Capt. Sully and co-pilot Jeff Skiles decided to do the unthinkable: **land the plane in New York's Hudson River.**

This was the first water landing jet in history, and Sully relied on his intuition and experience to make the decision. He deftly maneuvered the aircraft to a safe landing while processing the problem in his mind. All passengers were rescued to safety. The problem did not end there for Sully. The National Transportation Safety Board (NTSB) accused Sully of jeopardizing the lives of passengers by choosing to ignore the ATC's orders to return to La Guardia. Sully challenged the accusation **since he had a deep**

conviction that he had made the right decision and ultimately proved the NTSB wrong during the investigation.

Now, Sully's landing on the Hudson is called a "miracle," and his leadership abilities at a time of "life and death" have become lessons for leaders in management schools and are often cited by business leaders. In my opinion, calling the landing a "miracle" is an insult to Sully because Sully made some calculated decisions during the 3 minutes and 28 seconds, which is the time from when the birds hit the plane to the time Sully landed the plane on the Hudson. To me, the question is, **"What was the basis for Sully's decision? Was it intuition or logic?"** Often times, we rely on data to make decisions since we are overwhelmed with it, but in Sully's case, he couldn't have made mathematical computations using distance, speed, and time to make the decision.

Also, Sully followed Stoicism. Marcus Aurelius, the last of the Roman rulers known and a Stoic philosopher, said, **"The impediment to action advances action. What stands in the way becomes the way."** What he meant by this was that any obstacle can be used as an opportunity for creative problem-solving. So, when attacked by superior forces at unexpected locations, Aurelius did not resort to anger or panic but instead undertook a creative search for his available options. Sully did the same.

What an Octopus Can Teach Us

On the topic of learning from nature, one of the recent films that had a significant impact on me was *My Octopus Teacher.*

The documentary film captures a year spent by filmmaker Craig Foster forging a relationship with a wild common octopus in a South African kelp forest. While the relationship between humans and animals has always been an intriguing area to explore, it is often confined to domestic pets such as dogs and cats or friendly ones such as elephants and dolphins. Having said that, I agree that there are a number of videos on YouTube that show relationships that exist in the wild between mankind and animals, such as lions, tigers, leopards, etc. *What makes My Octopus Teacher special is the relationship that gets built between a man and an octopus and* **the lessons the octopus offers the man.**

Burned out by his work and suffering from depression, Foster explains early in the film that he was seeking a way to recharge and reconnect with his family when he started free diving near his home. It was during one of his first excursions that he spotted the octopus. Foster decided to visit the animal every day and, over a period of time, bond with it. Initially not welcoming, the octopus slowly let Foster into her world, where she slept, ate, and lived. Foster stayed close to her and observed how she defended herself from her predators, especially the

Pajama Sharks, whose favorite food is octopuses. In one attack on her, the octopus loses an arm and retreats to her den to recover, slowly regenerating the arm over 3 months. In another shark attack a few months later, she shows incredibly improved creativity to survive, including sticking to the shark's back.

While Craig Foster shares his learnings on the fragility of life and humanity's connection with nature using the octopus, watching the film taught me a few things:

Your teacher or mentor can come from anywhere, and there is no better teacher than nature. In ancient India, all learning happened in the **Guru-Sishya Mode**. But before the guru accepts the sishya, he tests him to see if the mentee is qualified. The octopus sort of does that here. She sees Craig as a threat, but after 3 months, she understands that he is not and allows him inside her world, which opens the gates of learning for Craig.

Every species has its own unique strength. During the first attack, the Pajama Shark chops and eats one of the octopus' arms while the octopus manages to save her life. But losing the arm makes her exhausted, and she completely slows down. The arm forms again for 3 months, after which she comes back in full force, but the 3 months is a long period of struggle, as she has to find food and stay alive by not leaving her den or making restricted movements as her predator also keeps looking at her outside her den. Like how nature has designed a unique strength for the octopus, which is the regenerative ability of her arm, every species has its own unique strength offered by nature.

Time is limited, but there is a purpose to life. A flower gets to live just a day. Probably, a male mosquito gets to live 10 days maximum from birth to death. Similarly, a giant octopus lives anywhere between 3-5 years; if at all, it survives all the attacks from predators. Again, octopuses can reproduce only once in their lives, and reproduction in the octopus world means death for both the male and female for reasons that are still being discovered. An octopus can lay anywhere between 50,000 and 100,000 eggs, but only 1% of them survive. What can the poor creature even do, given the vulnerability surrounding it? Those are the thoughts in our minds, but nature seems to have a purpose for every creature on earth.

Never give up: There are many instances in the film where most of us would have given up. For example, just as he is beginning to create a real connection with the animal, Foster accidentally drops his camera, which scares the creature, causing it to abandon its den and flee into the forest. As Foster notes, his task became searching for a creature that is known for being impossible to find. The natural, possibly more sane decision would be to give up. But Foster refuses to concede and instead spends a full week tracking the octopus.

The Obstacle is the Way: At one point, the octopus manages to travel with her predator, the Pajama Shark, by placing herself in the shark's back while the shark is actually searching for the octopus to kill and eat her. A stoic message from the octopus. 😊

What Penguins Tell Us About Teamwork

Have you watched the 2005 documentary film **The March of the Penguins**? This is a film that I often don't bring up at home because it talks about "men taking additional responsibilities at home." ☺. Jokes apart, the movie is about the Emperor Penguins and the lives of penguins in general.

The female emperor penguin lays a single egg and then goes to sea to feed, leaving the male to care for the egg. **The fathers survive the harsh arctic winter by huddling together to keep warm and incubate the egg.** The mothers don't come back until the dead of winter. By then, the chicks had just hatched. The mothers feed the chicks fish regurgitated from the mothers' stomachs. The fathers, not having eaten anything for more than 4 months, then have their chance to return to the sea. Before they leave, the fathers memorize the distinctive call of their chick so that they can later locate their own. Like the fathers, **the mothers now protect themselves from the cold and storm by huddling together.** When the fathers come back to the colony, they feed the chicks, and the mothers return to the sea. The parents take turns babysitting their chicks on the pack ice and returning to the sea to fish through December or January (the height of the Antarctic summer) when the chicks are large enough to fend for themselves. Any break in the chain (the death of a father or a mother or a delayed return) will spell the end for the chick.

Now, what does the arduous journey and life of the penguins teach us?

If we stay together, we will survive.

In the movie *Gladiator*, Russell Crowe, who plays Roman General Maximus Decimus Meridius, tells the other slaves during a fight, "If we stay together, we survive." In Antarctica, Emperor Penguins survive temperatures as low as -60 degrees and winds up to 100 mph by huddling together. This is a little odd for these penguins, as they are usually very territorial and will not approach each other easily. But without this huddling activity, the frigid cold would sap their energy, and they would die. So, it really is a good thing that they get over their territorial selves and work together to survive.

Humans can learn a lot about "teamwork" from penguins.

A Window to the Johari Window

When I initially started my career, I used to be aggressive (the hostile, belligerent type). One of my managers early in my career pointed this out to me during a feedback session, saying, "You are quite aggressive. Try and be assertive and not aggressive." I thought I knew everything about myself when someone told me about a trait of mine that I was not aware of. A few years later, I learned about the *"Johari Window."*

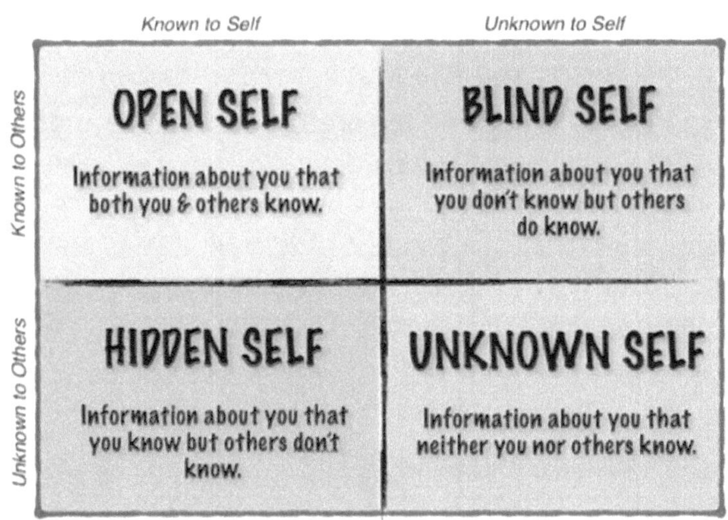

The Johari Window is a model of interpersonal awareness. It's a useful tool for improving self-awareness and, through it, our abilities to work well with others. It works by helping us understand the differences between how we see ourselves and how others see us. Invented by psychologists Joseph Luft and Harry Ingham (a portmanteau of their first names is why the name Johari) because ***they believed that what happens in our lives depends upon our own self-awareness and the awareness others have of us.*** The 4 regions of the Johari Window are as follows:

• What is known by the person about himself or herself and is also known by others is called 'open area, open self, free area, free self, or 'the arena.'

• What is unknown to the person about himself or herself but which others know is called a blind area, blind self, or 'blind spot.'

• What the person knows about himself or herself that others do not know is called 'hidden area, hidden self, avoided area, avoided self, or 'facade.'

• What is unknown by the person about himself or herself and is also unknown by others is called 'unknown, unknown area, or unknown self.'

One of the great advantages of organizations asking for 360-degree feedback is that it increases self-awareness. The feedback allows the individual to discover strengths, weaknesses, and ***particularly blind spots (behaviors and actions that they exhibit but are not aware of).*** Uncovering blind spots is key to continuous improvement and enables the employee to focus on developing skills in overlooked areas. Try the "Johari Window" when you can. In organizations, we can use it to try to increase the size of the "open area" compared to the rest of the quadrants, as it helps in better teamwork, collaboration, communication, and coordination.

Do you know who takes advantage of this window? Reputable screenplay writers use the "Johari Window" to build strong characters. I can give several examples, but films such as *Brokeback Mountain*, *The Blind Side* and *Finding Nemo* have some great scenes that demonstrate the 4 quadrants of the 'Johari Window.'

ChatGPT – Threat or Friend

My favorite bilingual writer, Jeyamohan, would always say, "Never pass comment on topics that are hot, for no one knows what happened. Allow time for things to settle down so that clarity can emerge." Now that the ChatGPT fever has reduced, let me share some thoughts. 😊

Recently, a client asked us what we are doing with "ChatGPT" at Zuci Systems, and I said we are cautiously exploring what it can do for us. Having spent time on Data Analytics and Machine Learning for 4 years now, we know how Artificial Intelligence systems work. Without the right inputs, no AI system can do what it is expected to do. Hence, there is no point getting excited about using ChatGPT unless we know how to use it effectively and get the best out of it for our needs.

Many years back, I watched the movie *Moneyball*. *Moneyball* is the real story of the Oakland Athletics, a baseball team, and their 2002 season. More than the team, it is about Billy Beane, the team manager who ***built a competitive team of players by taking a statistical approach (sabermetrics) to identifying and analyzing players***, which changed the game forever. Brad Pitt plays the role of Billy Beane in the movie. ***The reason I mentioned Moneyball was because it is about innovation.***

Billy Beane did not rely on AI-based systems but instead took help from Peter Brand (played by Jonah Hill), a young Yale economics graduate with radical ideas about evaluating players. Beane asks whether Peter Brand would have drafted him out of high school; though scouts considered Beane promising, his career in the major leagues was disappointing. Brand says he would not have drafted him until the ninth round and adds that Beane would've thereby turned down the Mets' offer and gone to Stanford on a full sports scholarship instead. Impressed, Beane hires him, and that paves the way for 'sabermetrics.'

Billy Beane used sabermetrics instead of relying on scouts to find and evaluate players. Usually, baseball teams were dependent on the skills of their scouts to find and evaluate players. Scouts are experienced in the sport, generally having been players or coaches. Oakland Athletics team's front office (read Billy Beane) took advantage of more analytical gauges (sabermetrics) of player performance to field a team that could outsmart and better compete against richer competitors in Major League Baseball. **Maybe AI models are being trained to deliver accuracy based on 'sabermetrics' today, but without Billy Beane and Peter Brand, there is no role for the AI models.**

Billy Beane was forced to 'innovate' given the circumstances. *Whenever we hear the word 'innovation', it sounds very complex and makes us all feel small because the word sounds like it is made for geniuses.* But as Tom Freston (Co-Founder of MTV) said, ***"Innovation is taking 2 things that exist and putting them together in a new way."*** I believe innovation is what differentiates us humans from other species. When VCR (Video

Cassette Recorder) entered homes in the late 70s, the movie industry was threatened, but it did not stop them from making movies. This fresh perspective opened a new business altogether. Similarly, when OTT platforms took center stage during the pandemic, the movie industry once again was threatened, but producers and directors got innovative and took huge advantage of the platform. Without OTT, we would have never watched some of the movies, for they would have never been made for mainstream 'the theaters.'

Rather than worrying about ChatGPT and other AI technologies taking our jobs, we need to find innovative ways to co-exist with such technologies and use them to our advantage.

What is your 7000 RPM Zone?

"There's a point – 7000 RPM – where everything fades. When your seeing becomes weightless, it just disappears. And all that's left is a body moving through space and time. 7000 RPM that's where you meet it. Can I ask you a question? The only question that matters. Who are you?" – Carroll Shelby, Ford vs. Ferrari (2019)

RPM stands for revolutions per minute, and it's used as a measure of how fast any machine is operating at a given time. In the movie *Ford vs. Ferrari,* Carroll Shelby calls 7000 RPM as that exhilarating moment during a race, which in miles per hour is about 91.7 and roughly translates to 147.5 kilometers per hour. The reason behind the name of the movie is that Enzo Ferrari refuses a merger of Ferrari with Ford, choosing Fiat instead, and sends some ugly insults to Ford. An enraged Henry Ford II issues an ultimatum to his staff: come up with ideas to beat Ferrari at races or be fired. Astronomical costs and high man-hours be damned, all he wants is for Ford to beat Ferrari at the world's most prestigious car race, the 24 hours of Le Mans.

The story builds up to the creation of an eccentric crew that builds the fastest Ford car, the GT 40 (and later the GT 40 Mk. II) — the legendary Lee Iacocca from Ford, Shelby and his engineering team, and the most eccentric of the lot, a brilliant Christian Bale as hot-headed but daring race car driver (and struggling mechanic), Ken Miles. When I watched *Ford vs. Ferrari*, there were many scenes that stood out for me, but the one dialogue above kept going through my mind for days. I asked myself, "What are those 7000 RPM moments for me in my profession?"

- Prospect meetings give me those 7000 RPM moments, especially tough ones where they challenge me or compare me with a competitor and ask why they should go with us.

- Solving a problem for a prospect and making an impression on them gives that moment.

- When a big deal gets signed after a long chase, a lot of consulting, and complexities involved, it gives those moments.

- Dealing with complex situations or tough clients is a 7000 RPM moment.

- Teaching someone something that I know and when they understand is one such moment again.

- Learning something new is a 7000 RPM moment.

The list can keep going, and without these 7000 RPM moments, there is no excitement. I am pretty sure that is the case for many of us. **What's your 7000 RPM zone?** One of the things I loved most about the film was how it explored its main theme—passion. Even if you're not into racing at all, you can understand the obsessive, blazing desire inside the hearts of these men. Being a creative, passionate pioneer often also requires you to be a stubborn, brazen, rule-breaking renegade and even make some sacrifices in order to do your very best work—ideas that the film seamlessly incorporated.

World of Speed Cubing

The Speed Cubers: This short 40-minute documentary focuses on 2 young men and the world of competitive speedcubing. Available on Netflix, the documentary captures the extraordinary twists and turns in the journeys of Rubik's Cube-solving champions.

The Sport is Fascinating: You don't see someone really solve a Rubik's Cube in just a few seconds and so quickly that their hands just become blurred. That's just one part of the beautiful documentary, but the real story is about the relationship between Feliks Zemdegs, former king of the cubers, and Max Park, a 17-year-old autistic boy, who is Feliks' biggest competitor and unlikely friend. There are a number of things to learn from this documentary, such as the effect of countless hours of practice (Grit), the ability of the human mind to store about 300 algorithms and identify patterns when solving a Rubik's cube in just a few seconds, pushing each other to get better and so on but more than anything, I felt the key takeaway from this documentary is the *constant endeavor to become a better version of yourself.*

Let Go of Limiting Beliefs: Max's emotional development is like that of an 8 - 9-year-old. He was formally diagnosed with autism when he was young. While the news was devastating to his parents, they always looked at the unique strength their son had instead of his challenges. When Max naturally gravitated toward a Rubik's cube at home, his mother learned to solve it using YouTube and taught him. The journey began there. For someone who couldn't use his fingers (and had a lack of fine motor skills in general), Max's parents spent tons of time in therapy to help him use his fingers.

Create Empowering Rituals: Great achievers develop habits that make them great. This could include fitness, eating healthy, getting good sleep, etc. We see Feliks recommending Max eat more greens, stay relaxed despite the pressure surrounding him as a champion, etc. Feliks helps Max get better by sharing all the input he needs while also knowing that Max is his biggest competitor.

Stay Positive: As we try to be the best version of ourselves, we are sure to hit roadblocks and obstacles. Instead of getting discouraged, we need to cultivate positive emotions. We see Max's parents helping him with the same. Max's emotional development doesn't allow him to accept failures. We see Max crying out loud after losing one of the competitions, but after a couple of years, we see Max coping with failure. Kudos to the parents for helping him understand how to stay positive.

Manage Yourself Effectively: Part of understanding how to be the best version of yourself is learning to be your own boss through effective self-management. Feliks understands that despite being a super cubing champion, it is not a career choice for him. He works in the Finance industry today while trying to practice cubing as much as he can.

Getting Out of Your Comfort Zone: To be the best version of yourself, one needs to live with no regrets. We need to get out of our comfort zone, take risks, and fail so that we can get back in and succeed. Feliks Zemdegs, the king of speedcubing, gets challenged by his new opponent Max Park, who always looks up to Feliks as his mentor. In fact, at one point in the documentary, Max's father says Max brushes his teeth at night before bed because Feliks does it. While constantly supporting Max as a friend and a great human being, Feliks constantly challenges himself by practicing for countless hours, identifying his weaknesses, and improving on them.

The Surgeon's Cut

Four specialists offer 4 different perspectives on life. *The Surgeon's Cut,* a docuseries, captures real stories and great insights for us.

Fetal medicine specialist **Dr. Kypros Nicolaides**, **Dr. Alfredo Quinones-Hinojosa**, a neurosurgeon, **Dr. Nancy Ascher**, the first woman to perform a liver transplant, and India's **Dr. Devi Shetty of Narayana Hrudayalaya** get featured. What makes the docuseries a compelling watch is the background of these surgeons, their approach toward the profession, and their philosophy of life based on personal experiences and from their profession.

To me, the most inspiring of the 4 was the story of Dr. Alfredo Quinones-Hinojosa, *who jumped borders from Mexico into the US, worked on farms picking vegetables/fruits in Fresno, California, before going to Harvard Medical School* to get his medical degree, accomplished so many other things academically and professionally, and went on to become a neurosurgeon at the Mayo Clinic in Florida. Like Andy in *The Shawshank Redemption*, **Dr. Alfredo's story is all about hope**. He was asked not to dream by fellow immigrants working on the farms, who were happy that they had moved to a new country where opportunities were available for them to make their lives better. On the other hand, **Dr Alfredo Quinones-Hinojosa dreams big and achieves it all.**

While Dr Alfredo's story was so inspiring, the story of Dr. Devi Prasad Shetty, who started "Narayana Health/Narayana Hrudayalaya" in Bengaluru, is the best of the lot as it shows how one man's vision can touch the lives of so many people. Dr. Devi Shetty has performed more than 16,000 heart operations and successfully performed the first neonatal heart surgery in the country in 1992. He believes that the cost of healthcare can be reduced by 50% in the next 10 years if hospitals adopt the idea of economies of scale. That's why Wall Street called him the "Henry Ford of Heart Surgery." Leaving aside the business aspects of healthcare, what truly stands out in Dr. Shetty's story is his idea of "Pay It Forward."

Toward the end of Dr. Shetty's episode "Heart and Soul" in the docuseries, he shares the letter that he wrote to all the 4000 children he operated on during his stay in Kolkata in which he asks, ***"Can you spend a few moments of your precious time for someone who needs it without expecting anything back in return?"*** Dr. Shetty says, "It is very important that when good things are done, they get documented so that future generations will read it and do the same or even something better."

I was just reminded of the movie *Pay it Forward*. Based on a novel of the same name by Catherine Ryan Hyde, the movie talks about the story of a social studies teacher who gives an assignment to his junior high school class **to think of an idea to change the world for the better and then put it into action.**

People With a Growth Mindset are Grittier

In the book *Mindset: The New Psychology of Success* by Dr. Carol S. Dweck, the author talks about how success in school, work, sports, the arts, and almost every other area of human endeavor can be considerably influenced by how we think about talents and abilities. Nobody is born with a fixed or growth mindset because everyone is born curious. It's just what *our parents, teachers, surroundings, and societies cultivate in our minds. People with a fixed mindset* believe that their or someone else's qualities, character, personalities, behavior, talents, shortcomings, etc., are fixed. *People with a growth mindse*t believe that your basic qualities, like personality, character, etc., are things you can cultivate through your efforts.

There is nothing wrong about having a "fixed mindset," but Dr. Dweck says that people with a *fixed mindset are less likely to flourish than those with a growth mindset – those who believe that abilities can be developed.* Mindset, she says, can be used by us to achieve outstanding accomplishments, citing examples from different walks of life. What are some examples of fixed and growth mindsets? The image below can probably help us understand.

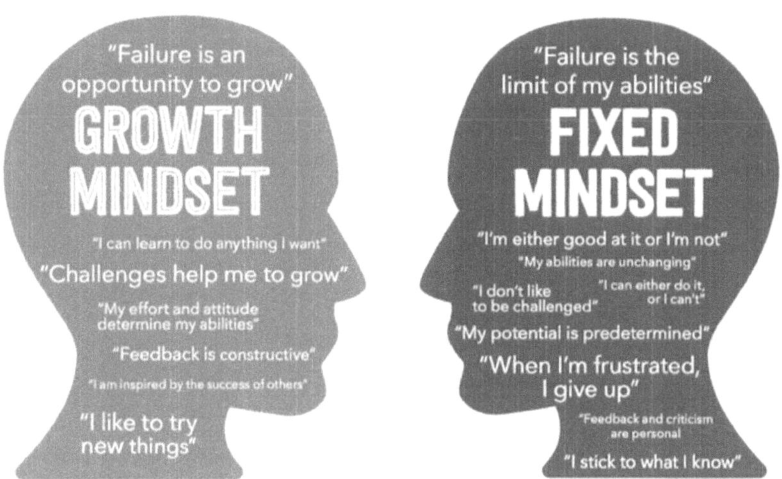

Several examples from different industries can be cited for the growth mindset. In the business world, leaders like Jack Ma (Alibaba), Elon Musk (Tesla and SpaceX), and Alan Mullaly (Ford) are great examples of having a "growth mindset." For example, Jack Ma says rejection does not mean failure and wisdom is important, which are qualities of a growth mindset. Similarly, Elon Musk is said to have learned about "rockets" by asking scientists to refer to books and reading them, which demonstrates "growth mindset" characteristics of "prioritizing learning over seeking approval" and "thinking of learning as brain training."

Talking about movies, *what do you think is common between Bambi, Simba, Cinderella, Snow White, Elsa and Anna, Maui, Lilo, and Kit Cloudkicker?* All these Disney movie characters are orphans, but in addition to being parentless children, their characters often display a growth mindset. In the movie

Forrest Gump, its protagonist is all about having a "growth mindset" demonstrating qualities such as "Your true potential is unknown," "You can grow your abilities," "Do not take anything personally," "Do not focus on consequences," "People with a growth mindset are grittier," and many more.

Homeless to Harvard

Khadijah Williams, a recognized advocate for homeless youth and a survivor has been homeless since the age of 6. She lived in and out of shelters, attending 12 schools in 12 years. Khadijah got into Harvard, and her Harvard acceptance story captivated many people, including celebrities like Oprah Winfrey, because it was all about "determination and focus." It can be cited as an example of Survival of the Fittest, not because she calls herself a "survivor" but since Survival of the Fittest refers to the fact that the 'fittest' can survive in any environment, regardless of its complexity.

Khadijah says, "Unfortunately, the reality of homelessness is chronic poverty, prostitution, and death," and it is rare for homeless people to escape, let alone get into college, let alone get into a place like Harvard. At one point, Khadijah was living in a shelter where she had to get up at 4:00 a.m. every day during her high school life to commute by bus so that she could continue to attend school. She says she knew that education was her ticket out of poverty—it was a matter of life and death. In her own words, "I think the most important thing that I did was to seek out help. I signed up for programming and enrichment opportunities for low-income students. I did every extracurricular activity I possibly could. I studied twice as hard as my peers because I had to."

Khadijah's life reminded me of the American actress and producer Viola Davis, who was not homeless but lived in abject poverty and dysfunction during her childhood. At 8 years old, she was chased home from school every single day by a group of boys who threw bricks at her and yelled racist comments. Despite all obstacles, Viola Davis succeeds. She says, "A more examined life is something everyone has to live if they want to stray out of the pack, and when you come to a race in deficit, which means you don't have the same tools as others, you still have to run the same race." When we feel down on our luck, we can feel helpless. But we're only helpless until we really try to help ourselves. While there is nothing wrong with asking for help from others, we should also try to rely on ourselves.

As Christopher Robin says in *Winnie the Pooh*, "You're braver than you believe, and stronger than you seem, and smarter than you think." 😊

What Do You Want to Achieve?

I follow Richard Branson, founder of Virgin Group, on LinkedIn and other social websites. Earlier this week, he shared his answer to a question that was recently asked of him. The question was, "Now that you're at the end of your life... what do you want to achieve"? Mr. Branson interrupted the questioner and said, "Hold on a minute! Let me answer the first part of the question. **I feel I am in my prime.** I live healthily and am fitter than I have been in many decades. Now, I'm 71 years old and fully aware of it. But I put a lot of effort into my fitness, managed my diet well, and tried to keep a healthy balance in my life, and my parents happily both lived long into their nineties. **I've got a lot of life left to live.**" Now, that brings us to the second half of the question: What do you want to achieve? There is often lots of talk about leaving a legacy for people in the second half of their lives, but I prefer to think about what there is left to achieve. **I have never been a fan of looking back, and I love to look forward to what is coming next.**

Richard Branson's answer reminded me of my teacher and favorite bilingual (Tamil, Malayalam) writer Jeyamohan, who once, in a speech, said in Tamil, "ஒருபோதும் சென்றடையயவில்லை என்கிற நிறைவின்மையை அடைக" which roughly translates to **"Always carry the lack of satisfaction inside you that I have never reached my destination."** It's a complex line and a frustrating one because all that we humans aim for is to get somewhere and reach some kind of destination. **Why should I think I am never going to reach my destination?** Because once that satisfaction arrives, **you feel there is nothing left to do after this.**

Once again, the movies are a great source to look for those who live with this approach that Richard Branson talks about. At 91 years of age, Clint Eastwood directed *Cry Macho* in 2021. When asked about retirement plans and aging, he said, "I'd like to be a bigger and more knowledgeable person 10 years from now than I am today. I think that for all of us, as we grow older, we must discipline ourselves to continue expanding, broadening, learning, and keeping our minds active and open." At 81, Al Pacino continues to act, as do actors like Robert De Niro and Joe Pesci, who are both 79 years old. Our own Amitabh Bachchan is in his prime at 80 years old, doing a couple of movies a year and shows like KBC. What is left for these people to achieve? Why do they keep going? I don't know. Maybe, as someone said, **"Sometimes, the best way to learn is to go beyond limits and set your own rules."**

Filmy Funda - If our net worth is estimated at 500 crores, would we do this when we are 66 years old? 😊 (You can find the QR code to the video in the last section of this book, titled 'Watchlist Library')

The Artistic Crime of the Century

"When I see 3 oranges, I have to juggle them. When I see 2 towers, I got to walk." – Philippe Petit.

On the morning of August 7th, 1974, Philippe Petit gained fame for his walk between the Twin Towers (yes, the ones that were the target of the September 11th, 2001 attack) of the World Trade Center in New York. Yeah, high-wire walk is a big deal, but there are people who are skilled at it. So, what is special about Philippe Petit? **Well, this one was unauthorized.** What does that mean? It means Philippe did not get any kind of permission from New York authorities to perform this high-wire walk, and that means all his preparations were secretive. How is that possible?

While waiting to meet with a dentist in 1968, Philippe Petit saw a photo of the WTC Twin Towers in a magazine. Analyzing it, he dreamed of doing a tightrope walk between them. He decided to travel to America, setting the date for the walk as August 6, 1974. What was called the "artistic crime of the century" took Petit 6 years of planning. During this period, he learned everything he could about the buildings and their construction. In the same period, he began to perform high-wire walking at other famous places.

The Twin Towers were under construction during that time, and Petit and his crew entered the towers several times and hid on the upper floors and on the roofs of the unfinished buildings to study security measures. They also analyzed the construction and identified places to anchor the wire and other things. Using his own observations, drawings, and photographs, Petit constructed a scale model of the towers to design the needed rigging for the wire walk.

Working from the ID of an American who worked in the building, Petit made fake identification cards for himself and his collaborators (claiming they were contractors who were installing an electrified fence on the roof) to gain access to the buildings. Prior to this, Petit had carefully observed the clothes worn by construction workers and the kinds of tools they carried. He also took note of the clothing of office workers so that some of his collaborators could pose as white-collar workers. He observed what time the workers arrived and left so he could determine when he would have roof access.

On August 7th, 1974, shortly after 7 am, Petit stepped out on the wire and started to perform. He was 1,350 feet above the ground. He performed for 45 minutes, making 8 passes along the wire, during which he walked, danced, lay down on the wire, and knelt to salute watchers. There was extensive news coverage and public appreciation of Petit's high-wire walk. The district attorney dropped all formal charges of trespassing and other items relating to his walk on the condition that Petit give a free aerial show for children in Central Park. The Port Authority of New York and New Jersey gave Petit a lifetime pass to the Twin Towers' Observation Deck. Petit's high-wire walk is credited with bringing the Twin Towers much-needed attention and even affection, as they had initially been unpopular. Many critics had regarded them as ugly and utilitarian in design and too large a development for the area. The Port Authority was having trouble renting out all of the office space.

"It's the possibility of having a dream come true that makes life interesting. And, when you want something, all the universe conspires in helping you to achieve it." – Paulo Coelho, *The Alchemist.*

Big, Beautiful, Blank Sheet of Paper

Last year, my younger daughter told me about a teacher of hers who awarded marks for an answer that was actually not the "expected" one. It looks like this teacher asked my daughter to come and meet her during break and asked the reason why she responded with that choice of answer. My daughter explained her reasoning, and at the end of it, the teacher seemed to have said, "Your thinking is right, and going by your thinking, your answer cannot be labeled as wrong. Hence, I am going to give you marks for this." I told my daughter that I would like to send a handwritten note to her teacher because I learned something from her today and also because what she did was on the same lines that great educators like Marva Collins, Rafe Esquith, and Dorothy DeLay did.

Marva Collins taught Chicago children who had been judged and discarded. For many, her classroom was their last stop. Most children (4th and 5th graders) who came to her class could not spell their names but ended up reading Shakespeare and other literature meant for high schoolers and above. Great teachers believe in the growth of intellect and talent, and they are fascinated by the process of learning. **The same applies to leadership.** What is common between Jack Welch (General Electric), Lou Gerstner (the man who saved IBM), and Anne

Mulcahy (the woman who brought Xerox back to life)? They all started with a ***belief in human potential and development – both their own and others.*** Instead of using the company as a vehicle for their greatness, they used it as an engine of growth – for themselves, the employees, and the company as a whole. True self-confidence is "the courage to be open – to welcome change and new ideas regardless of their source," and that's what great leaders carry.

In my experience, I have seen organizations spend a lot of money every year trying to teach leaders and managers how to coach their teams, provide effective feedback, identify and nurture talent, and so on. However, much of this training is ineffective, and many leaders and managers continue to remain poor coaches. Why? Research sheds light on the reasons. "Many managers do not believe in personal change. They judge employees as competent or incompetent at the start, and they carry that image forever." Without a belief in human development, corporate training programs become an act of formality and are done to use the budget given to Learning and Development. Many organizations believe in natural talent and don't look for people with the potential to develop.

Jumping into the field of acting, there is hardly talk of "natural talent." One of the greatest actors of all time, Marlon Brando, says, "All actors, I believe, arrive eager and alive but dumb. They don't really understand anything outside of their desire to act, to be seen, to be understood, and to bring understanding to others. I was particularly dumb because I had come from a background with a habit of expression, of acting out, of feeling and thinking things, and I did not have a foundation in literature, philosophy, art, or music. I was a big, beautiful, blank sheet of paper, as Stella (his acting coach Stella Adler) told me, and it was my job to impress some notes and thoughts on this blank page–to make an impression. She would help me, she said, but she could not make it happen; she could not make me into an actor; she could not make me sensitive or intelligent. What she could do, she said, and what she emphatically would do, **was kick me out of her class and her life if I did not subscribe to her standards, did not appear to be working at my highest potential, or if my page remained blank.** She was a tough, brilliant, and beautiful teacher. She taught me everything." **As we can see, Stella Adler was not just an acting teacher or coach but a leader.**

A Doctor and Not A Nurse

I have a friend of mine who is a doctor here in the US. During a recent meeting, we were discussing the topic of gender bias, and she said, "I wear a tag in the hospital that says I am a doctor and not a nurse." I was surprised to hear that and asked her why. She said visiting doctors, new peers who join the hospital, and patients often think women are mostly nurses and are not doctors. This is because she is brown-skinned, and many Indian women work as nurses in the US, Canada, and other countries. She said race is one thing, but in general, women doctors, irrespective of race, lack recognition.

What my doctor friend said reminded me of interesting data that I recently read. In 1970, women made up 38% of all US workers and 8% of STEM (Science, Technology, Engineering and Math) workers. By 2019, the STEM proportion had increased to 27%, and women made up 48% of all workers. So, men made up 52% of all US workers but 73% of all STEM workers. In essence, despite making up nearly half of the US workforce, women are still vastly underrepresented in the STEM workforce. If this is the scenario in a developed nation like the USA, we can imagine how it would be in other countries.

Dr. Carol S. Dweck, in her book *Mindset: The New Psychology of Success* says, "A fixed mindset, plus stereotyping, plus women's trust in other people's assessments of them contribute to the gender gap in the field of STEM." What does that mean? Dr. Dweck gives examples.

Frances Conley is one of the most eminent neurosurgeons in the world. In fact, she was the first woman ever given tenure in neurosurgery at an American medical school. Yet careless comments from male colleagues – even assistants – could fill her with self-doubt. One day during surgery, a man condescendingly called her "honey." Instead of returning the compliment, she questioned herself. "Is a honey," she wondered, "especially this honey, good enough and talented enough to be doing this operation?" Dr. Dweck says, "Even when women reach the pinnacle of success, other people's attitudes can get them."

I have seen this in my experience, too. Early in my career, I have seen friends of my gender not being open to 'women writing good computer codes' and would always say, 'There is a better way to do this.'

Being a film buff, whenever I search for examples, films jump in front of me. Here we go: The 2016 film *Hidden Figures* captures the true story of 3 African-American female mathematicians (Katherine G. Johnson, Dorothy Vaughan, and Mary Jackson) who worked at NASA during the Space Race. Set during a time of racial and gender inequality, the film tells the untold story of the 3 females' achievements, which restored the nation's confidence during the 1960s. The film focuses on several real-life people, in addition to including some fictional characters to help drive the storytelling. The movie has several lessons to offer, such as "the power of mentors," the power of teamwork," "women advocating for women," "pushing to advocate for yourself," "having true grit," and so on. A must-watch!

The Power of Deliberate Practice

Angela Duckworth, the author of *Grit: The Power of Passion and Perseverance*, says, "Grit has 2 components: **Passion**, which is based on a sense of purpose, and **Perseverance**, which means sticking with one's mission even when the going is tough."

Pravin Tambe's story exemplifies grit. Tambe made his Indian Premier League debut at the age of 41, becoming the oldest-ever IPL debutant. He had no experience playing professional cricket prior to his IPL debut.

I used to watch cricket, but after the 2011 World Cup, I didn't follow the game in any of its formats. So when my friends recommended that I watch the video of Rahul Dravid talking about a player named Pravin Tambe, I didn't give it much attention. But after seeing the trailer for *Kaun Pravin Tambe,* I went back and saw Rahul Dravid's talk. And I was so inspired when I learned about Pravin Tambe and his story. **Why is Pravin's story special?** Too often, we attribute success to talent alone, and when we think of talented people, **we think of those with a natural ability.** Pravin Tambe was no natural but put in "deliberate practice," a key element of grit, to reach his goals.

What is "deliberate practice"? Deliberate practice refers to a special type of practice that is purposeful and systematic. While regular practice might include mindless repetitions, deliberate practice requires focused attention and is conducted with the specific goal of improving performance. Deliberate practice ends up improving your skills. You analyze everything you do during this phase. You get feedback mainly on what you are doing incorrectly. And finally, you make adjustments, try again, and repeat the process. In other words, what people often attribute to talent is actually the result of a lot of deliberate practice.

In the world of quality, we talk about **"Kaizen (continuous improvement)."** Angela Duckworth uses the phrase "Kaizen" in her book when talking about deliberate practice. It's not just about what we are doing; it's about how we can make it better. Rahul Dravid found the same about Pravin Tambe - Pravin was always looking to improve and get better.

"Nobody wants to show you the hours and hours of becoming. They'd rather show the highlights of what they've become," says Duckworth in her book. Rahul Dravid says, "Pravin was not an overnight success. It was 25 years of effort that helped him become a success." Duckworth and Dravid are saying the same in their own ways. Isn't it?

Insulated Bubble

On his first day as CEO of the Carlsberg Group, a global brewery and beverage company, Cees 't Hart was given a key card by his assistant. The card locked out all the other floors for the elevator so that he could go directly to his corner office on the 20th floor. And with its picture windows, ***his office offered a stunning view of Copenhagen.*** These were the perks of his new position that spoke to his power and importance within the company. Cees spent the next 2 months acclimating to his new responsibilities. But during those 2 months, he noticed that he saw very few people throughout the day. Since the elevator didn't stop at other floors and only a select group of executives worked on the 20th floor, ***he rarely interacted with other Carlsberg employees***. Cees decided to switch from his corner office on the 20th floor to an empty desk in an open floor plan on a lower floor. When asked about the changes, Cees explained, **"If I don't meet people, I won't get to know what they think. And if I don't have a finger on the pulse of the organization, I can't lead effectively."**

The story above, shared in the 'Harvard Business Review,' is an excellent example of how one leader actively worked to avoid the risk of insularity that comes with holding senior positions. And HBR said this risk is a real problem for senior leaders. In short, the higher the leaders rise in the ranks, the more they are at risk of having an inflated ego. And the bigger their ego grows, ***the more they risk ending up in an insulated bubble, losing touch with their colleagues, the culture, and ultimately their clients.*** An unchecked ego can warp our perspective or twist our values.

Oliver Stone's movie ***Any Given Sunday,*** starring Al Pacino, Jamie Foxx, Dennis Quaid, and Cameron Diaz offers some interesting insights into how a star football player's ego affects a team before he realizes his mistake and becomes a team player. Flashy, unproven 3rd-string quarterback Willie Beamen, played by Jamie Foxx, is the last hope of a struggling, injury-depleted fictional football team, the Miami Sharks. Failing to win his first outing using his coach Tony D'Amato's (played by Al Pacino) conventional plays, Beamen rebels against the system, opting to call his own with victorious results. As the Sharks' chances of making the playoffs increase, so do those in charge of the media, who grow infatuated with Beamen's high-risk, high-reward style. With the spotlight hovering above the charismatic quarterback, Beamen's ever-expanding ego began to demand more lights, especially camera lights, for his rap music video "My Name is Willie." He fails to recognize his girlfriend's true love and pushes her out of his life. His cocky behavior infuriates his teammates and coach, who eventually bench him due to his ungracious behavior. Humbled, mature, and genuinely apologetic, Beamen returned to the starting position when the Sharks needed him most.

What is the quick take?

Similarly, in an organization, being a team player is as important as not being carried away by superstardom within a business unit or across the org.

Dot Style

Rosalind Roz Chast is an American and staff cartoonist for *The New Yorker*. Since 1978, she has published more than 800 cartoons in *The New Yorker*. In the book *Grit: The Power of Passion and Perseverance*, there is a section where Angela Duckworth captures rejection in the life of cartoonists after hearing Roz Chast speak at a local library in New York. Roz Chast, 68 years old and a celebrated cartoonist, shares that at this stage in her career, her rejection rate is 90%. ***If she sends 10 cartoons to The New Yorker for publishing, only one will get published.*** Angela Duckworth, who says she was shocked to hear Roz talk about her rejection rate percentage in the life of professional cartoonists, wanted to validate it and hence called **Bob Mankoff,** the cartoon editor for *The New Yorker*, and was even more shocked when Bob responded saying, "Roz Chast is indeed an anomaly since most cartoonists live with even more rejection."

At *The New Yorker,* contract cartoonists, who have dramatically better odds of getting published than anyone else, *collectively submit about 500 cartoons weekly*. In a given issue, there is only room, on average, *for about 17 of them*. Did you do the Math? **That's a rejection rate of more than 96%**. While Angela Duckworth wondered who would keep going when the odds were that grim, she says she found the answer in Bob Mankoff himself. **Bob Mankoff's story is all about dogged perseverance.** Bob Mankoff was rejected by *The New Yorker* **2000 times between 1974 and 1977** before the cartoon posted above sent by him was accepted.

How did Bob handle rejection and move ahead? As children, we were told, "**Try, Try, and Try Again. If something is not happening, keep working until it happens,**" and things like that. It was not very different for Bob Mankoff. The piles of rejection slips from *The New Yorker*, however, suggested to Bob that "try, try again" was not working. *He decided to do something different.* Bob went to the New York Public Library and looked at all the cartoons from 1925 that had ever been printed in *The New Yorker*. He first thought he did not draw well and was getting rejected, but he saw that some very successful New Yorker cartoonists were average. Then Bob thought that something might be awry with the length of his captions (too short or too long), but that was not an issue either. He wondered if his type of humor was missing the mark, but no. He saw some successful cartoons as whimsical, satirical, philosophical, and enjoyable.

However, the one thing all the cartoons had in common was this: they made the reader think. And there was another common thread: Every cartoonist had a personal style that was distinctively their own. There were only so many best styles. **Paging through literally every cartoon *The New Yorker* had ever published**, Bob knew he could do as well. Or even better. "I thought, I can do this, I can do this, I had complete confidence." He knew he could draw cartoons that would make people think, and he knew he could develop his style. **"I worked through various styles and eventually did my dot style."** The now-famous dot style of Bob's cartoons is called 'stippling,' and Bob had initially tried it out back in high school when he discovered the French impressionist Georges Seurat. What followed next was interesting. He sold *13 cartoons to The New Yorker in 1978, 25 the following year, and 27 the next year.* In 1981, Bob received a letter from the magazine asking if he would consider becoming a contract cartoonist. He said, **"Yes."**

Connecting the dots can reduce the rejection rates.

Filmy Funda - There is a scene in the Tamil movie Mugavari and it is something I watched when I used to feel low during my early years. (You can find the QR code to the video in the last section of this book, titled 'Watchlist Library') Before Ajith Kumar started churning out no logic, loud-mouthed dialogues in movies 😊, I used to like him for his choice of stories and as a director's actor. I started my career around the same time (maybe a couple of years later in 1998/99 as Vijay, Ajith, and Surya) in IT, so I consider them my peers and have taken inspiration from them, mostly from Surya, who has shaped his talent and career with sheer hard work. 😊

Keep Moving. Fall Forward.

LinkedIn and other professional social media websites have been filled with information about layoffs in EdTech, FinTech, and many other SaaS startups for the past few months. We see people blaming the companies for the debacle and complaining about valuations, work culture, termination policies, etc. Not that there is no truth in what people are saying, but getting fired doesn't mean it's the end of the road.

So far, I have seen 2 economic downturns in my career. The first economic collapse happened when I was in Singapore in May 2002. I was 23 years old then. I was hired as a PHP developer on contract for a travel/tourism website company. On the third day after I joined the employer, I heard my manager talking to my agency about how bad my code was and why they needed a replacement for me as soon as possible. *I was 3 days into the job when this happened.* I had hardly written 50 lines of code for their email server. I was asked to leave work on the 4th day afternoon, and with no employment opportunities in Singapore due to the 9/11 crash that had happened a few months earlier, I returned home to India with no job in hand but with an ongoing home mortgage EMI and a 1000 Singapore dollar loan, that I took from my cousin to book air tickets from Singapore to India.

The second was the 2007-2008 financial market crash. I returned from London to Chennai in July 2008 to be with my wife, who was pregnant with our second child. The market crash led to the closing of the account in London that I was working for, and my company placed me on the bench in India. I was born a hyperactive kid, and sitting on bench was not something for me 😊. *I was looking for action all the time.* The market worsened and downsizing continued in my company, but I knew I was safe. However, I couldn't take the boredom of being on the bench and decided to quit first and then look for a job. I thought the two-month notice period would be reasonable for me to find one. With utmost confidence in my abilities and the notice period duration, I submitted my resignation one morning, only to hear the company tell me that evening that I could be relieved in 2 weeks since they wanted to save money given the dark economic conditions. *This time, a home loan, one kid in kindergarten, and one about to enter the world in 2 months.*

I did not intend to talk about my life this week and brag about it 😊 but I wanted to share my experience because it depends on how you look at things. I could have fought in Singapore, saying, "I was never given time to understand the codebase, and it was unfair to fire me," or gone for a never-ending discussion on the "notice period clause," but *I thought these were happening for my good.* Looking back, I am happy I got to experience these. Had I not returned from Singapore, I would have never learned "Software Testing" because when I took a job as a Java developer in Chennai after returning from Chennai, that company also ran out of Dev work, and I was moved to Testing. Had I not left Hexaware, I would have never known Venky, Anil, and Zuci would not have happened. 😊 Steve Jobs had once revealed in an interview *that getting fired from Apple was the best thing that could have ever happened to him.* The board decided to fire Jobs after a rift between him and the then-CEO John Sculley. Interestingly, he was fired on September 16, 1985, and was hired back the same day, 12 years later. Sometimes, we have to step back or pause a bit to go and do bigger things.

An economic downturn is not new. Layoffs and firing are not new. They were always around. It is just that they are all so much in the news these days and the way we perceive them. Most big companies were built during the economic depression of the 1930s. *General Electric, General Motors, IBM, Disney, HP, Hyatt, FedEx, and Microsoft all started during a recession.* Though technically not started during recessions, Google, Salesforce, and Facebook were all launched right before major economic meltdowns: Google (1998) and Salesforce (1999) were right before the dot-com bubble burst, and Facebook (2004) was shortly before the Great Recession. Having weathered the storms, these 3 companies posted a combined $72.77 billion in revenue in 2019 alone. If one wants to be an entrepreneur, there cannot be a better time than now.

Winston Churchill said, **"The pessimist sees difficulty in every opportunity. The optimist sees opportunity in every difficulty."** I am not saying you should dream when reality hurts, but there is much to do with how we view a problem.

True Dedication

The day was December 18th, 2006. Karnataka and Delhi played in the Ranji Trophy tournament at the Ferozshah Kotla in Delhi. Karnataka had posted 446 in the first innings and reduced Delhi to 103/5 with 2 young boys named Virat (batting at 40) and Bisht (batting at 28). The day's game ended, and Virat went home tired. His world would change that night as his father, Prem Kohli, passed away due to a cerebral attack during the wee hours of December 19, 2006. Mithun Manhas was leading Delhi and had become reconciled to the fact that the first innings lead was hard to achieve. "I normally reach Kotla at 7.45 AM, but I don't know why I was at the stadium gate 15 minutes earlier than my routine. When I reached the dressing room, I saw Virat sitting (on the bench in the corridor) and holding his head. I was worried," remembered Manhas. "What's wrong, beta?" asked Manhas. "I lost my father," the youngster mumbled. "I was shocked and honestly did not know how to react," Manhas recalled. "This was a situation I had not experienced. There were just the 2 of us in that corridor, and I looked around for a while to see if I could get someone to help comfort the boy. There was no one."

Manhas asked Virat to go home, but the latter responded promptly, "I want to play." The Delhi captain asked, "Why? Why do you want to play?" "Sir, the atmosphere at home is heartbreaking. My family and coach also want me to continue with my innings. They have sent me to play," Virat told him in a matter-of-fact manner. "I was stunned by the boy's dedication even in this hour of grief," said Manhas in an interview. Virat went out to bat and radiated such confidence at the crease that his batting partner Bisht was inspired to give his best. Bisht made 156 in that game, but Virat was dismissed when batting at 90 because of a questionable "caught behind" umpiring call. He headed for the crematorium from Ferozhshah Kotla.

Starting with Mithun Manhas, the Delhi Ranji team, Delhi coach Chetan Chauhan, and the 2 umpires PS Gobole and MSS Ranawat, everyone who came to know about the tragedy couldn't fathom how Virat padded up and looked normal under the circumstances. For Virat, it was a way of paying tribute to his father, who had always supported his ambitions to be a cricketer. The sportsman within gave Virat the courage to face this irreparable personal tragedy, and he was off to the Ferozeshah Kotla to continue with his knock that had halted with the day's play at 40. Delhi was in a difficult position, and here was a youngster trying his best to save his team from embarrassment while overcoming such monumental grief at home. Virat's discipline had admirers in the Karnataka camp, too. For Venkatesh Prasad, former seamer of the Indian team and the coach for Karnataka during that tournament, it was the second time he watched a teammate return to the cricket field from his father's funeral. In 1999, Sachin Tendulkar showed a similar commitment at the World Cup in England. "It was a very emotional moment. We were not even aware that Sachin had flown back home for the funeral. India's performance against Zimbabwe was terrible, as it suffered a loss that shocked the fans. Tendulkar joined the team for the next match against Kenya and came up with a century in Bristol as a fitting tribute to his late father. For coach Venkatesh Prasad, Virat's act was exemplary grit and dedication.

"True grit is making a decision and standing by it, doing what must be done. No moral man can have peace of mind if he leaves undone what he knows he should have done." - John Wayne

An Inspiration Called Mandela

Nelson Mandela's leadership style is an important lesson to me since it demonstrates how to unite diverse people despite adversity.

Once, during his time in prison, he was able to unite fellow prisoners who had differences and work toward a common goal of ending apartheid (According to Wikipedia - Apartheid was a system of institutionalized racial segregation that existed in South Africa and Southwest Africa from 1948 to the early 1990s.)

How did Mandela do it - Mandela intervened to mediate a peaceful resolution when a conflict between 2 groups of prisoners was on the verge of becoming violent by listening to both sides and identifying points of agreement.

What can we learn from this? What was Mandela's conflict resolution mantra? Simple – intervene before it blows up big. Listen to both sides, identify the points of agreement, and reach a consensus.

This exemplifies the value of empathy, active listening, and finding common ground to accomplish a shared objective. Most conflicts in the workplace and in families can be resolved by using Mandela's method.

"There is no passion to be found playing small - in settling for a life that is less than the one you are capable of living." - Nelson Mandela.

This is one of my favorite quotes by Nelson Mandela. As I recollected Nelson Mandela's quote, I was reminded of the movie *Invictus*. *Invictus* was directed by Clint Eastwood, and the movie shows how Mandela used the 1995 Rugby World Cup as an opportunity to unite and inspire a racially divided South Africa. There are several great movies on leadership, and Invictus is one of them. The film is based on the book ***Playing the Enemy: Mandela and the Game that Made a Nation*** by John Carlin. The movie, which is based on true events, ***shows how leaders can make change real with self-confidence and optimism***. Mandela believed he could heal the wounds of oppression and unite a country through tolerance. He also thought that sport — especially rugby — could play a big part in helping him achieve his goal.

One of my favorite scenes from *Invictus* is Nelson Mandela (played by Morgan Freeman) asking Francois Pienaar (played by Matt Damon), the captain of the Springboks (South African rugby team), "What is your philosophy of leadership?" The captain replies that leading by example is his philosophy of leadership. Mandela says that's right ***but then asks how to inspire people and tell them they can do better than they are***. He says people need to be inspired by others, and they need something to cheer for and draw inspiration from. **A poem. A song. A team that is unified and puts all else aside for the goal of victory.** He then talks about his time in prison at Robben Island, where things got worse, and how he used the poem "Invictus" to inspire himself. Francois Pienaar gets the message, and his team wins the 1995 Rugby World Cup.

Mandela's message of peace, love, and unity continues to inspire people of all ages and backgrounds. He was a true hero, and his contributions to the world will never be forgotten.

Scoreboard

I had some friends who played cricket at the first division level (Jolly Rovers, India Cements) in Chennai, and through them, I had a chance to meet with former Indian cricket players like Sadagopan Ramesh and Lakshmipathy Balaji a few times in the past. Many years ago (2004, I guess), during a meeting with my cricketer friends in 'Mayajaal' - which at the time was one of Chennai's trendiest spots - L Balaji joined us at the table since my friends had invited him. I think he was part of the Indian team back then. Balaji, being a celebrity, drew crowds to our table, and he acknowledged everyone with a smile, signed autographs to those who asked for them, spoke to every kid in awe of him, and finally, we got some time to speak with him. Needless to say, his down-to-earth attitude and friendly nature truly inspired me, and he had absolutely no airs about his celebrity status. But this post is not about L. Balaji. ☺

As we started talking, one of our friends at the table asked Balaji about his experience sharing the dressing room with players like Sachin Tendulkar, Sourav Ganguly, and others. Balaji shared a few things about them, and there was one thing he said about Sachin Tendulkar that caught my attention. Balaji said, "Sachin has a scoreboard for himself. Whether he gets out in the 40s, 50s, 100s, or 200s, Sachin would always introspect every ball he played during the innings. Not that he was nit-picking or indulging in perfectionism, but it's just that he had higher standards of performance that he set for himself to adhere to." Those words just stuck to me.

In Ryan Holiday's book *Ego is the Enemy*, he shares the characteristics of how great people think. In his own words, "It's not that they find failure in every success. They just hold themselves to a standard that exceeds what society might consider to be objective success. Because of that, they don't care much about what other people think; they care whether they meet their own standards. And these standards are much, much higher than everyone else's." And he shares all this in a chapter aptly titled 'Maintain your own scorecard.' We see this 'scorecard approach,' with almost everyone wanting to keep doing better and not set mediocrity as a standard. They are in every industry. Kamalhaasan, Roger Federer, Maniratnam, Virat Kohli, M.S. Dhoni, Sanjay Subramaniam, Thotta Tharani, Ravivarman, Martin Scorsese, Quentin Tarantino, Anurag Kashyap, the list goes on. You will never see these names deliver anything below the standard they have set for themselves.

No mediocrity, just excellence, and only excellence.

Mistakes Happen

I am sure many of you would have watched the movie *Saving Private Ryan*. The movie's ensemble cast comprised Tom Hanks, Matt Damon, and others. Directed by Steven Spielberg, the film is based on the real story of the Niland Brothers.

Saving Private Ryan deals with much emotional content but also teaches us much about **teamwork, trust, leadership, navigating chaos, vulnerability, situational leadership, and other qualities.** Led by Tom Hanks as Captain Miller, a squad is put together by the US Army during the middle of World War II to save Private Ryan (Matt Damon) and send him home since they fear that all 3 brothers of Ryan have died in the war, and he is the only one left for his parents. The team led by Captain Miller is a disparate bunch who are upset that they are being sent to find, protect, and send one person home in the middle of the war while they can do a lot for the nation.

As the leader of the squad, Captain Miller demonstrates extraordinary leadership. For instance, the war has impacted his physical health, leaving him with hands that are constantly shaking. But instead of trying to cover that up, he exposes his vulnerability to the squad, who understand that he is also like them, facing the pressures of the war, trying to do the best he can and not be superhuman. This **builds *trust and collaboration*** within the unit. We spoke about how ***vulnerability builds trust*** in a meeting last week, and I am sure the ones who attended the session can connect to this.

For a significant part of the movie, the squad doesn't know Captain Miller's background, and he doesn't reveal much about him despite being asked by different squad members. At a very intense moment, though, Miller decides to break his silence and diffuse a situation that's about to escalate and burst. As his squad prepares to break the rules of war by executing a prisoner, Miller reveals that he used to be a teacher. Suddenly, ***the normality of Miller's homelife amplifies the insanity of the situation***. He's not a superhero built with iron but a regular guy with a wife, home, career, and daily worries. ***Remember, you're not a machine; your team needs to know you are also a real and normal person.***

When Miller's squad knows that their purpose is to save Private Ryan, they are not happy. Why waste the lives of an entire unit to save one person? A sergeant in the team tells a squad member that he is not pleased about this, and the team member says he feels the same. Slowly, everyone in the squad shares the same feeling. ***Rather than join in with the complaining of his men, Miller refuses.*** In a brilliant moment of communication, he outlines the rules of complaining in the US Army. **"I don't gripe to you Reiben. I'm a captain,"** he says. **"There's a chain of command. Gripes go up, not down. Always up. You gripe to me, I gripe to my superior officer, so on, so on and so on."** It's a rule that applies to all business teams. It can be easy for a middle manager to complain about his bosses to his team, but it always has a negative impact. **You might disagree with what**

you're being asked to do, but if you join the complaining, it undermines the leadership of your whole business, including yours.

Desperate to find Private Ryan so he can complete his mission, Captain Miller fails to do his due diligence with the first/wrong Private Ryan they meet. The conversation becomes a disaster as Miller tells Ryan that his school-age brothers have been killed in combat. It's a massive mistake, but Miller doesn't avoid it. As Ryan begins to cry, Miller admits there's been a huge mistake. Sometimes, even the most experienced and thoughtful leader can get things wrong; the secret is to accept it. **Getting things wrong is often the first step toward getting things right.**

When it comes to leading his men in battle, Captain Miller doesn't shy away from danger. He's not the sort of commander to take a back seat while his troops are in the firing line. *As a frontline leader, you've got to lead from the front.* Prove to your team that you're willing to step into the firing line, and you'll win their respect.

Passionately Curious

She was called Pattee at home and was born on June 22, 1960, in Kansas, USA. In 1981, Pattee won the Miss Pacific Coast beauty pageant and married her first husband, Shawn Brown, in 1982. They had 2 children. After their divorce in 1987, Pattee became a secretary at a brokerage firm. There, she met and married her second husband, Steven Brockovich, and they had a child together. However, the marriage only lasted a year, and they divorced in 1990. After a bad traffic accident in Reno, she moved back to California, where her career as a legal assistant began. Pattee, better known as Erin Brockovich, convinced her lawyer, Ed Masry, to give her a job as a file clerk in his law firm, Masry & Vititoe. ***Here, Brockovich stumbled upon medical records that would lead to the largest direct-action lawsuit in US history.***

"The important thing is not to stop questioning. Curiosity has its own reason for existence. I have no special talents. I am only passionately curious." – Albert Einstein.

Despite no knowledge or education in law, Erin Brockovich was instrumental in building a case against Pacific Gas & Electric Company (PG&E) involving groundwater contamination in a town called Hinkley in California, with the help of attorney Ed Masry in 1993. The case was settled in 1996 for $333 million, the largest settlement ever paid in a direct-action lawsuit in United States history. Masry & Vititoe, the law firm for which Brockovich was a legal clerk, received $133.6 million of that settlement, and Brockovich received $2.5 million as part of her fee. The lawsuit was the subject of the Oscar-winning film *Erin Brockovich*, starring **Julia Roberts as Erin Brockovich**. Erin Brockovich was a single mom, and she needed work. She did what was needed to help her children have food on the table. **What can we learn from Erin Brockovich's life?**

Self-confidence: Erin had loads of self-confidence. Right from joining, she was confident she could deliver despite not knowing what a law firm does.

Self-belief: "I have no legal expertise, but I will do everything I can to bring justice for these people." says Julia Roberts, who acted as Erin Brockovich in the movie.

Love what you do: The law firm that Erin worked for took another big law firm's support to fight PG&E. One of my favorite scenes in the movie is - where the larger firm tells Erin, "Her research has gaps." Erin asks what information they want, and the law firm says some of the Hinkley resident files need phone numbers. Erin asks, ***"Whose numbers do you need?"*** They challenge Erin, asking for a resident number, and Erin gives the entire history of the resident and their disease details. For a law firm, the lawsuit was their job, but for the real Erin, she loved what she did, empathized with every member of the town of Hinkley, and connected with them like a family.

Be clear about what matters to you: Erin told her boyfriend, George, ***"If you're my man, you need to accept how important my work is, and I won't choose between you and my work."***

Even when she is at the risk of losing George, Erin's intentions and priorities are clear. She has 3 children to attend and, at times, has taken them to Hinkley with her. It was extremely hard for her as a single mother, but as a tough and strong woman, she had clarity on what she wanted.

Net and Gross

I recently read an interview with a world-famous CEO, and here is an excerpt from it.

"I was 50 years old when I was having a board meeting, and by then, we were maybe the largest private group of companies in Europe, and I asked the question when somebody gave some figures, ***"Is that good news or bad news?"*** One of the directors took me out of the room and said, "Richard, I've known you for years now, I've never really dared ask you, but am I right in thinking you don't know the difference between net and gross?" And I said, ***"Well, I've never been able to admit it, but yeah, that's the case."*** He pulled out a sheet of paper, and he had some crayons and he colored the piece of paper blue and he said, "That's the sea." Then he put a fishing net and some fish in the net, and he said, "The fish that are in the net, that's your profit at the end of the year, and the rest of the sea is gross turnover." **I have name-dropped net and gross ever since.** I realized that Virgin's net worth is nowhere near as big as I thought it was." **Yes, the entrepreneur was Richard Branson of Virgin Group**, who has 400 companies under his belt.

I follow Richard Branson on LinkedIn and read articles about him because he exudes so much hope and positivity. As many of you might already know, Richard Branson was dyslexic and didn't know he had dyslexia until his twenties. Yet, Branson is convinced that his dyslexia has made him a better businessman *because he has an original perspective, is more innovative, and is willing to take risks.* In his own words, "I've never seen myself as an entrepreneur; *I've seen myself as a creator. I'm not really interested in making money per se; I'm interested in the things that I create surviving. It doesn't really matter if you failed elementary Math's, as I did at school all those years ago. Somebody else can add up the figures. I've just got to deliver a product that exceeds expectations. Take Virgin Atlantic—38 years ago, we flew with one second-hand 747 across the Atlantic. Everybody thought we were mad. We were taking on British Airways with 300 planes. If I'd gone to the accountants and asked them to do some figures to see whether it was a good idea to go into the airline business, they would have told me, 'You'll never survive.'"*

Actors and filmmakers are similar to entrepreneurs like Richard Branson. Most of them lack formal education or minimal education but are very confident in themselves and what they are capable of. Complete "vibrant and positive" people who generate so much optimism and energy, which drives their teams to achieve the vision. Director of famous movies like *Titanic* and *Avatar* James Cameron once said, *"Pick up a camera. Shoot something. No matter how small, no matter how cheesy, no matter whether your friends and your sister star in it. Put your name on it as director. Now you're a director. Everything after that you're just negotiating your budget and your fee."*

The Barrier

Recently, when I met a client of ours, they said, "Vasu, your team does great work, but we often don't know what they think because they don't speak much. We have left everything for your team to own, and when they don't speak, you can imagine the challenges we have." From straining relationships to endangering lives, communication has the power to inflict severe damages when not correctly done. I know many of you must be now thinking "How can communication put life at peril? I find this exaggerating."

In Malcolm Gladwell's book *Outliers,* there is a chapter called **"The Ethnic Theory of Plane Crashes."** Gladwell looks into the history of plane crashes and Korean Air in this chapter. He talks about how communication is crucial for flying. ***Gladwell analyses 2 major plane crashes and gets to the bottom of why the planes went down. He also digs deeper into how cultures and customs play a role in the cockpit.*** A Korean Air (now Korean Airlines) flight crashed into a hillside in Guam due to many factors. The weather was rainy and foggy. The pilot was also fatigued since he had been up for nearly 20 hours. In addition, a large spotlight called a glide scope, which is used to help guide pilots to the runway, was being repaired. Because the glide scope was down, the pilot had to use a VOR. It sends a signal to the plane and guides the plane down. Sometimes, the VOR station isn't at the airport like the one in Guam. The one in Guam is on the side of a hill 2.5 miles from the airport. The pilot knew this yet may have forgotten due to his lack of sleep. The plane crashed into Nimitz Hill, 3 miles southwest of the airport, ***killing 228 of the 254 people on board***. The other crew members knew the captain was doing the wrong things **but did not speak up**. Together as a team, they could have helped the pilot during the bad weather. But they didn't. Why? Poor Communication. **In Korean culture, you don't challenge the boss and his/her thoughts. It's like a family hierarchy where you respect elders. Questioning them is considered rude. So, the entire team kept silent. And where did it lead to? Loss of 228 lives.**

Delivering projects is like flying an aircraft, except the duration is much longer. The Project Manager is the captain of the flight. The manager needs support from the entire team. Team members need to speak. They need to highlight challenges, question the status quo, and work together as a team to make sure the captain (project manager) is on the right path. ***The PMBOK (Project Management Body of Knowledge) says 90% of projects fail due to "lack of communication" and not for any other reason.*** The topic of communication always reminds me of director Alejandro González Iñárritu's movie *Babel*. Babel is a film about communication, mainly listening. There are 4 main storylines, which involve 4 countries and 5 languages. However, the director uses a rifle to link the 4 stories together aptly, which makes it a coherent movie.

The first storyline is about a married American couple, Richard and Susan. They travel to Morocco, but Susan is shot and injured during the journey. The second storyline is about 2 brothers who live in Morocco, one of whom unintentionally shoots Susan. The third storyline is about a Mexican woman named Amelia. She is the babysitter of the Richard family. The last one is about a deaf Japanese girl, Chieko. Chieko desperately wants to be loved and to be cared for. Babel is peculiarly suited to give meaning to intercultural concepts, as its 2 central themes are culture and communication. In mythology, The story of Babel in Genesis recounts man's effort to become equal with God and build a tower that reached the heavens. ***God, angry at man's arrogance, confounded man's communication with different languages.*** On the other hand, **the movie *Babel* is a profound work about the human condition of not listening and the consequences of the misunderstanding that follows.** This movie, however, suggests that it is not the barrier of language that creates humanity's lack of communication but the barrier of not listening and not loving.

Build Without Ego

One of the questions that Baradwaj Rangan asked Maniratnam in his Wide Angle interview was, *"You always chose to work with the best minds in the industry. Earlier, it was "Ilaiyaraja-Maniratnam-Thottatharani-Lenin-Vijayan-P.C.Sriram" and now it is "ARR-Maniratnam-Ravi Varman-Thottatharani-Sreekar Prasad-Ekha Lakhani. How do you work with your collaborators? Is it like, 'Either you convince me, or I convince you?' How does it work? How easy is it working with them?"*

I will come to what Maniratnam answered later, but Baradwaj's question reminded me of a chapter from the book *Ego is the Enemy* by Ryan Holiday. The chapter is titled **'BEWARE THE DISEASE OF ME.'** Ryan Holiday says, "For us, it's beginning to think that we are better, that we are special, that our problems and experiences are so incredibly different from everyone else's that no one could possibly understand. It's an attitude that has sunk far better people, teams, and causes than ours." I often think how N.R.Narayanamurthy and his team of 6 other founders worked together for so long despite each one being capable of running their own companies. Whether **Nandan Nilekani, Shibulal, Kris Gopalakrishnan, Dinesh, N.S.Raghavan**, look at what they have accomplished, and you can identify an entrepreneur in each. The simple thing is whether it is my ego at play all the time or I am genuinely concerned about what matters to the organization.

And that was Maniratnam's answer, too. *"I really get top technicians. I trust them and they trust me. Together, we try to find something. And I take the responsibility. But if they are not convinced with what I am saying, I will listen to them, take their idea and give it a shot. If I am still not ok, I will return to what I am doing. But I think invariably we have been in sync. Sometimes their idea might open a new door for me and they often go with me because I am carrying everything about the film. I have the fuller picture. It's a nice balance. In Ponniyin Selvan, there it a lot of Ravi Varman, Thottatharani and Sreekar in the film. That's why I bring them. They better be there."* I wondered how different this is from what we do at Zuci.

We have leaders who are our top technicians. And then there is the entire workforce under them, who are again great technicians executing things based on the vision the management has working with the top technicians. Just like Ravi Varman's cinematography team, Thottatharani's art design team, or ARR's music team, who are the unsung heroes, we have ours too. ***The management has a fuller picture of where Zuci wants to go and what we want to do, but without this entire team of technicians, what would the management do?*** And what we are doing is we are constantly seeking ideas and thoughts from these top technicians. And these top technicians look for thoughts and ideas from the great team of technicians under them. And then what? We are striving for balance. We are trying to see what works and which ones should we pick up and go. We are also directing a 'Ponniyin Selvan' here, except we are doing a much longer version☺ And without a team of great technicians working together, doing the balancing act, not letting our egos come in between, how will the end product turn out?

As Ryan Holiday says, what matters in the exercise is, **"Let's make one thing clear. We never earn the right to be greedy or pursue our interests at the expense of everyone else. To think otherwise is not only egotistical, it's counter-productive."**

ZNDB taught me 3 essential pointers about life

- **Life is all about living in the present.** Given the unpredictable nature of life, it is important to live in the moment instead of worrying about the future or regret about the past. **Make the most of today.**

- **Work isn't everything.** Take a break and have some fun. It helps you.

- **Embrace your fears** instead of avoiding them.

Zindagi Na Milegi Dobara (ZNDB) is a Hindi film and remains one of my favorites on my list of inspiring movies.

A movie that I watched recently, *The Secret Life of Walter Mitty*, reminded me of ZNDB. In the film, Walter Mitty (Ben Stiller) is like most of us. He dreams of achieving big things, but his reality is the opposite – a 'normal' guy who struggles to win the girl of his dreams and finds it hard to recall anything that he has done noteworthy in his life. However, when faced with a real-life test, he goes on and achieves and exceeds everything he could have dreamed of.

I found one quote from the film very inspiring. Walter Mitty's colleague and heroine of the film says, **'Life is about courage and going into the unknown.'** Courage is often portrayed as ordinary people placed in extraordinary circumstances doing things beyond what they are capable of. A mother fighting a snake or leopard to save her son/daughter or a small boy jumping into fire to save his friends comes to as WhatsApp forwards exemplifying courage. But most of us will never face these situations to see whether we can be just as courageous. However, *we all face daily opportunities to be bold*.

Speaking confidently in a customer call and presenting our thoughts, taking a sales call, answering questions on pricing slides in a proposal to the prospect, handling production code changes, challenging a decision made by someone that we think can be better, learning a new skill, exploring unknown terrain, setting fitness goals all involve courage and most of us accept and do it as part of living our lives. **Courage does not have an off or on switch.** *All of us are courageous*; we simply have different levels of risk that we are prepared to take. So, next time when we are confronted with a situation *where the best action to take makes us feel uncomfortable,* rather than seeing it as an outlier event, let us recognize it as a point on the line between those risks that we are happy to take and those that we are not. **And then step into the unknown.**

In 2002, I was working in Zhuhai, China, a place located very close to Macau (Las Vegas of the East) and Hong Kong. Unlike now, flights were not always full back then, and Cathay Pacific operated at least 10 flights in the Hong Kong – Singapore sector every day. You can come into Hong Kong airport and take a Cathay Pacific flight to Singapore if you have a ticket. There is no need for prior check-in and all. I once planned a trip to Chennai from Hong Kong through Singapore, and I assumed that Air India would also operate like Cathay Pacific. I went to the Air India counter after reaching Singapore airport and asked for a seat on the next flight to Chennai (AI operated about 4-5 flights every day from Singapore to Chennai). Air India informed there were no seats on flights to Chennai for the next 48 hours. I was stuck at Changi Airport in Singapore.

I was frustrated for a while, but the 23-year-old in me was always ready for an adventure☺, took it in my stride, and started thinking of ways to spend the next 48 hours. In the next few hours, I made friends with other passengers (from different nationalities) who were stranded like me at Changi, and we spent the next 2 days together. I had very little money, and I still remember the warmth and kind acts of people who bought me food and helped me with other things. I will never forget the 2 days I spent at Changi. If 2 days could be so challenging to spend at an airport, think about Mehran Karimi Nasseri, an Iranian refugee who lived in the departure lounge of Terminal One at Charles de Gaulle Airport from 26 August 1988 until July 2006. His autobiography was published as a book, *The Terminal Man*, in 2004. Nasseri's story inspired the 2004 film *The Terminal*. I am sure many of you have watched it.

While the ***power of perseverance in the face of obstacles*** makes *The Terminal* a heart-warming and memorable film, It is also a film about 'communication' and, more importantly, 'empathetic communication.' **Empathic communication** involves both accepting and allowing different perspectives and emotions in other people and also sharing them with them to enable encouragement and support. It's also the ***practice of actively listening in an effort to understand the emotions of who you're communicating with***. The Terminal shows how Viktor Navroski (Tom Hanks) finds it difficult initially as an outsider who is stuck in the New York 'JFK' Terminal but gains enough grip on a foreign language to communicate with people in the airport and even hold a job. His pronunciation and grammar are imperfect, ***but Viktor never shies away from communicating what he thinks or feels***. In fact, he helps a man transport medical pills for his father because Viktor loves people and empathizes with other people.

A lot of times, we are worried about our diction, pronunciation, grammatical errors we make, etc., but honestly, all that doesn't matter. ***If we want to communicate something, we should just go for it.*** With time and practice, we will get better. ***Effectively communicating ensures that we not only convey our message to someone but also let them know about our feelings and emotions.*** Whether it is among family members, friends, clients, or colleagues, effective communication helps us get through the tasks of life with ease.

Your Move, Chief

I am often asked, "What is my take on Working From Home (WFH)?" It's a sensitive topic, and anything you say can be interpreted at the convenience of the listener or reader. One thing I have always wondered though, is if you stay at home, **where do you get your experiences?** Parents, Family? Fair point. But is that enough? In his book *The Case of the Bonsai Manager*, R. Gopalakrishnan devotes a chapter to 'Learning through coaching' with various examples. My favorites from them are: 'The Falcon and the Arab' and 'J.R.D Tata and John Peterson.'

The Falcon is a ferocious bird that Arabs train for hunting. The instructional training involves getting the bird to return to its perch on the Falconer's fist after the hunt. In Arabia, it takes them only 3 weeks to train the bird, which is half the time compared to other countries in the Middle East. Gopal says, "The Falcon never parts company with its master. The trainer carries the bird wherever he goes, communicating with it all the time in one way or the other – f*eeding it, stroking it, even holding conversations with it*." He says, "The emotional bond between the 2, called coaching or mentoring, accelerates training greatly." **Management literature is full of this theme.**

In another section on the same topic of "coaching," Gopal gives examples of Krishna-Arjuna from mythology, Helen Keller and Anne Sullivan, Michael Klein and his grandfather Max, and

J.R.D. Tata and John Peterson. When 21-year-old J.R.D.Tata arrived in India in 1925; his father took him to Peterson's room. "John," he said, "you know my son Jehangir. I would like you to look after my little boy." J.R.D. recalled that a small desk was ordered by Peterson to be placed in a corner of his room. Peterson never had a moment of privacy after that because every single paper going to his desk was routed through young J.R.D. (***recall the Falcon, which was always next to the Arab!***). Read Gopal's book to know more about this relationship and how Air India came into existence, for which John Peterson played a vital role (unknowingly, of course) by supporting his protégé start the airline. ☺

I think coaching cannot happen beyond a certain level in the work-from-home world. We need to learn from experiences, and they are available only from mentors we identify and associate ourselves with. One of my favorite movies on this topic is *Good Will Hunting*. In 1997, Robin Williams starred in the critically acclaimed *Good Will Hunting*. He played a psychologist with a troubled past who helped a young protégé, Matt Damon. The famous Park Bench scene (to me, it is the Oscar Moment) sums up the role of a coach.

The Toughest Race

The most painful marathon in the world takes place in the Sahara Desert in Southern Morocco. It's called '**Marathon des Sables**,' French for 'marathon of the sands.' It's a six-day, 156-mile-long ultramarathon, equal to 6 regular marathons. Each year, over 1,000 runners participate. But in 2022, *only 40 made it to the finish line*. Runners face threats in the desert, including dangerously hot sand, venomous snakes, scorpions, and steep sand dunes. The terrain sometimes becomes rocky, testing athletes' mental and physical fortitude. You can watch *Human Playground*, a documentary on Netflix, to learn more about Marathon des Sables. The first episode of the documentary, titled 'Breaking the Pain Barrier,' focuses on Amy Palmiero-Winters, a.k.a Amy, who became the first female amputee to complete the Marathon des Sables, known as the toughest foot race on earth.

Amy has a personal reason for taking part in this dangerous race. Amy wanted to be an athlete. She wanted to join the military. But when she was 19 years old, she was hit by a car on her motorcycle. The accident crushed her left leg below the knee. Forty-five surgeries later, her leg was amputated. Amy says, *"They told me I would never walk. They told me I would never run. Not many of us get a second chance, but I did. My gift is the ability to endure. I can never get stronger if I don't*

continue to challenge myself." And that's what led Amy to the Marathon des Sables. Amy's pain is a reminder of the obstacle she has overcome. For her, the Sahara Desert symbolizes the battle with the pain she faces daily. There are 3 other stories in this episode which completely bowled me over. Particularly the one with Dutch diver ***Kiki Bosch***, who plunges to extreme depths in the world's coldest waters as a form of therapy, that helps her to deal with the trauma of sexual assault.

As I watched the series, I wondered why humans do these extreme things in different walks of life. For instance, Howard Hughes, Steve Jobs, Elon Musk, Amy, and Kiki Bosch. Why do they do what they do? The documentary also answers that. Idris Elba, who narrates the documentary, says, ***"Working on the documentary project helped open his mind to what people can accomplish. You might be able to just go for a walk and walk further than you've ever done before. But in your own way, you can push yourself. You can expand."***

Synopsis

Random Takes is a compelling exploration of the intersection between the captivating narratives of cinema and the practical realities of corporate leadership. Authored by Vasudevan Swaminathan, Founder and CEO of Zuci Systems and a seasoned storyteller, this book delves into the transformative power of storytelling within the business world.

Drawing from a rich tapestry of films spanning various genres and eras, *Random Takes* takes readers on a thought-provoking journey behind-the-scenes of cinematic masterpieces. Through insightful analysis and engaging anecdotes, Swaminathan reveals the intricacies of storytelling techniques employed in filmmaking, highlighting their relevance and applicability in corporate settings.

Each chapter of *Random Takes* explores a different aspect of storytelling, from character development and plot structure to themes of resilience and innovation. Through compelling examples and real-world case studies, Swaminathan demonstrates how these storytelling principles can inform and enhance corporate strategies, leadership approaches, and team dynamics.

Whether it's learning from the leadership prowess of characters like Michael Corleone in *The Godfather* or the innovation-driven mindset depicted in *The Social Network*, readers will discover actionable insights and innovative approaches for navigating the complexities of modern business.

Ultimately, *Random Takes* serves as a valuable resource for leaders and professionals seeking to leverage the emotional resonance of storytelling to inspire change, foster collaboration, and drive organizational success. With its blend of cinematic allure and corporate wisdom, this book offers a fresh perspective on leadership and business strategy, inviting readers to reimagine their approach to leadership through the lens of their favorite films.

Disclaimer

The book "Random Takes," is a compilation of insights and analyses that have been developed through extensive research. While creating this work, I have engaged with various informational resources, notably the Internet Movie Database (IMDb) and several blogs authored by leading film critics. It is important to note that specific segments of the content presented in "Random Takes" may have been influenced or directly derived from the information obtained from these external sources. Readers should be duly informed of the potential for such external contributions to the content.

Watchlist Library

Dear Readers,

Thank you for checking out my musings on life, movies, business, and everything in between. To add some extra depth to what you've read, I've put together a bunch of videos that I think will help you dive even deeper into these topics. I have organized them by chapter, so just scan the QR codes to access the content.

Happy Watching!

WATCHLIST LIBRARY

1. Enable. Empower. Exemplify.

2. What Matters More: Chalk or a Clean Slate?

3. Stay in Character And Get Remarkable Outcomes

4. Hope is a Good Thing, and No Good Thing Ever Dies

5. Do Emotions Oppose Rational Thought?

6. Happy Endings

7. Coma to a Masterclass

8. What Can Brick Walls Teach Us?

9. When We Change Our Attitude, Sparks Fly in the Universe

10. Strength is More Mental Than Physical

11. Who You Surround Yourself With Matters

12. Intuition or Logic?

13. What an Octopus Can Teach Us

14. What Penguins Tell Us About Teamwork

15. A Window to the Johari Window

16. ChatGPT – Threat or Friend

17. What is your 7000 RPM Zone?

18. World of Speed Cubing

19. The Surgeon's Cut

20. People With a Growth Mindset are Grittier

21. Homeless to Harvard

22. What Do You Want to Achieve

23. The Artistic Crime of the Century

24. Big, Beautiful, Blank Sheet of Paper

25. A Doctor and Not a Nurse

26. The Power of Deliberate Practice

27. Insulated Bubble

28. Dot Style

29. Keep Moving. Fall Forward.

30. True Dedication

31. An Inspiration Called Mandela

32. Scoreboard

33. Mistakes Happen

34. Passionately Curious

35. Net and Gross

36. The Barrier

37. Build Without Ego

38. ZNDB Taught Me 3 Essential Pointers About Life

39. Your Move, Chief

40. The Toughest Race